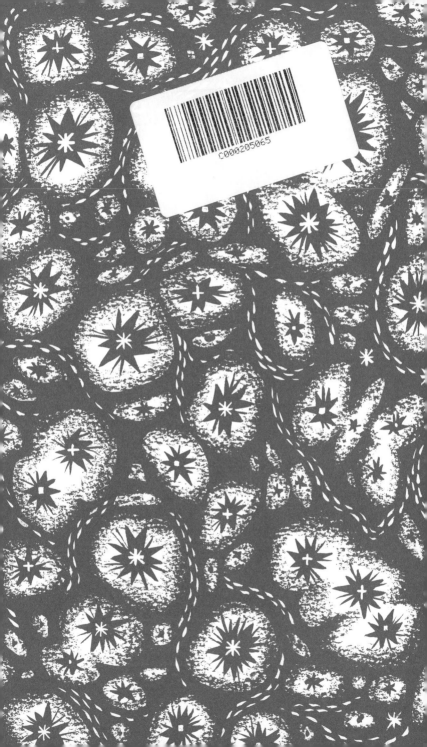

C000205065

Fiona Sampson studied at the universities of Oxford, where she won the Newdigate Prize, and Nijmegen. She has published sixteen books, including poetry, translations and studies of writing process, of which the most recent is *Rough Music* (2010). Her awards include a Cholmondeley and she is a Fellow of the Royal Society of Literature. *Music Lessons: The Newcastle Poetry Lectures* were published in 2011.

PERCY BYSSHE SHELLEY
Poems selected by FIONA SAMPSON

faber and faber

First published in 2011
by Faber and Faber Limited
Bloomsbury House, 74–77 Great Russell Street, London WC1B 3DA
This edition first published in 2011

Printed in England by CPI Mackays, Chatham

A CIP record for this book is available from the British Library

ISBN 978–0–571–27430–7

10 9 8 7 6 5 4 3 2 1

Contents

Introduction

When Percy Bysshe Shelley drowned off the coast of northern Italy, on 8 July 1822, he was still a month shy of his thirtieth birthday. In the course of his short life he had toyed with founding a utopian community, advocated atheism, republicanism and free love, become a vegetarian and an internationalist, married into one of the foremost intellectual families of his day, and fathered at least six children.

This seems so much of a piece with Romantic myth that it's easy to forget the extent to which Shelley chose the course his life took. His anti-tragic imagination resisted those forces, 'Lawyers or priests, a motley crowd', as he says in *The Mask of Anarchy*, which he saw as encouraging, or even enforcing, personal passivity. He was not a victim of destiny, and nor would such a role have interested him. Instead, a preoccupation with agency is at the very centre of his work, which returns repeatedly to the moment of change, and the puzzle of what makes that happen. A focus on action, and consequently responsibility, led him consistently to the boundary between private and public concerns, where thought, experiment and advocacy meet as what we would now call radical practice.

The pattern seems to have been set by the time he arrived at Oxford. In the first three months of 1811 he met both his first wife, the sixteen-year-old Harriet Westbrook, and Thomas Jefferson Hogg, the fellow undergraduate with whom he wrote and disseminated a tract on *The Necessity of Atheism*. This flamboyant gesture, in an era when faith was no private matter, got Shelley sent down from university and ended his plans to follow his father into parliament. Apparently unfazed, he eloped with Harriet to Edinburgh, where they were married that summer.

Ten years later, when he was twenty-eight, Shelley would complete 'Epipsychidion', the poem which perhaps best illustrates how entangled his emotional and intellectual lives were. Written at the time of his involvement with a young woman,

Teresa Viviani, whose father was bent on an arranged marriage, the poem fantasises escape to a life *à deux*. But Shelley also brings the range of his experiences – which by then included two marriages and a formal experiment in free love – to bear on 'those poor slaves' of monogamy, who 'With one chained friend, perhaps a jealous foe, / The dreariest and the longest journey go'. This apparent paradox contradicts the 'happy ever after' our twenty-first-century sensibilities have come to expect, but it's entirely in keeping with the poet's own fascination with change itself, caused on this occasion by love's 'flight of fire'. 'Epipsychidion' is also an example of the way intellectual and political preoccupations pressed Shelley's poetry into the service of advocacy, here of free love though elsewhere of wholesale social revolution.

Indeed, although he wrote traditional love lyrics, albeit often in expanded forms – such as the group of late poems 'For Jane' Williams – Shelley frequently transposed romantic occasions into philosophical puzzles about how to live. The late lyric 'When Passion's Trance is Overpast', for example, seems to be negotiating what its narrator would settle for, at the same time as he more conventionally declares its absence:

> When passion's trance is overpast,
> If tenderness and truth could last,
> Or live, whilst all wild feelings keep
> Some mortal slumber, dark and deep,
> I should not weep, I should not weep!

That double take is characteristically Shelleyan. The lyric mode may be confessional, but here what's personal includes not only the reactive register of feeling but active desires and decisions which can get to work in the world. As twentieth-century rhetoric might have it, *the personal is political*. It's not surprising that Shelley's poetry is sometimes engaged in a kind of self-invention we recognise reading back from, say, Allen Ginsberg's *Howl*, or the Adrienne Rich of *Diving into the Wreck*. In the extended self-portrait 'Letter to Maria Gisborne', for all its conversational tone and the intimacy of its allusions, the twenty-seven-year-old appears fully aware of the effect he's having, both publicly:

> And here like some weird Archimage sit I,
> Plotting dark spells, and devilish enginery,
> The self-impelling steam-wheels of the mind
> Which pump up oaths from clergymen, and grind
> The gentle spirit of our meek reviews
> Into a powdery foam of salt abuse,
> Ruffling the ocean of their self-content;—

and privately:

> Next winter you must pass with me; [. . .]
> Though we eat little flesh and drink no wine,
> Yet let's be merry: we'll have tea and toast;
> Custards for supper, and an endless host
> Of syllabubs and jellies and mince-pies,
> And other such lady-like luxuries,—

in a rather stagey form of self-invention.

How far could he go with these kinds of strategies and remain within the lyric tradition? Readers can find the occasionally homiletic note frustrating, even if it characterises some of Shelley's best-known lines:

> Lift not the painted veil which those who live
> Call Life: ('Sonnet')

> All things are sold: the very light of Heaven
> Is venal;   (*Queen Mab*, V)

> An old, mad, blind, despised and dying king,—
> Princes, the dregs of their dull race, who flow
> Through public scorn,—mud from a muddy spring,—
>   ('England in 1819')

On a hasty reading such passages seem clunkingly unassimilated to any lyric impulse. But pause to read them in context, as part of a flexible line of thought, and something else becomes apparent. These are the points where overt reasoning, as opposed to pure description or expression, comes to the fore – in a way that mimics how we do in fact think. Their very abruptness resembles 'having an idea'. Through this mimicry, they bring us face to face with a poetic *persona* that is attempting to resolve the essential tension within Wordsworth's idea of the poet as both exceptional and everyman.

In *A Defence of Poetry* (1821), Shelley amplifies William Wordsworth's famous formulation, in his 1802 Introduction to the *Lyrical Ballads*, that: 'the poet is chiefly distinguished from other men by a greater promptness to think and feel without immediate external excitement, and a greater power in expressing such thoughts and feelings'. For Shelley, that requires a near-spiritual refinement:

> Poetry is the record of the best and happiest moments of the happiest and best minds. [. . .] A Poet, as he is the author to others of the highest wisdom, pleasure, virtue and glory, so he ought personally to be the happiest, the best, the wisest, and the most illustrious of men.

Though this articulation came late in his life, Shelley does seem to have lived, accordingly, with a certain conscientious sweetness. In the months immediately after Oxford he moved between Dublin, Devon, Wales and London, pamphleteering and struggling for money. It was while fund-raising on behalf of the utopian community of Tremadoc, for example, that he met one of his intellectual heroes, the anarchist utilitarian William Godwin, widower of Mary Wollstonecraft, with whose daughter Mary Godwin Wollstonecraft he would elope two years later.

But first, in 1813, he was to become a father, and publish a limited edition of his verse-play *Queen Mab*. This allegory on the revolutionary nature of individual responsibility eventually became notorious enough for the Chancery Court to deny Shelley custody of his son and daughter from his first marriage, after their mother Harriet had killed herself in 1816. Though both these children reached adulthood, only one of the four born to his second wife Mary would do so. Shelley was further named as the father of a seventh child, Elena, who also died in infancy. Infant mortality was high in the early nineteenth century, but in recent years these deaths, together with Harriet's suicide and that of Mary's half-sister Fanny, have sometimes been taken to symbolise the cost of the unsettled, chaotic life the Shelley circle led. This may be unfair; but avowedly engaged poetics lay the poet open to *ad hominem* criticism. It was after all Shelley himself who wrote that, 'A Poet, as he is the author to others of the highest wisdom, pleasure, virtue and glory, so he ought personally to be [...]'; and when a poet claims that the way he lives is the source of his poetic authority, questioning that lifestyle must be a legitimate way to question his whole poetic project.

Either way, with *Queen Mab* Shelley's poetry overtook his prose as the disseminator of his ideas. Its revolutionary themes made it a natural for pirate editions: there were two in 1821 alone. Shelley objected to these, writing that 'I regret this publication, not so much from literary vanity, as because I fear it is better fitted to injure than to serve the cause of freedom'; but they undoubtedly facilitated the book's adoption by the Chartist movement, and so by later Shelleyite social philosophers including George Bernard Shaw, Henry David Thoreau and Mahatma Gandhi, as well as German anti-fascists of the 1930s including Theodor Adorno, Walter Benjamin and Bertolt Brecht. Friedrich Engels may have been referring to these editions when he claimed, in *The Condition of the Working Class in England in 1844*, that most readers of 'Shelley, the genius, the prophet, Shelley' were 'in the proletariat: the bourgeoisie owns only castrated editions'.

Such public significance, though, would be largely posthumous. The poet's counter-cultural role – and, doubtless, his later exile in Italy – meant that relatively little of his large output had been published by the time of his sudden death. Meanwhile, intimate relationships continued to play a defining role in his life. His first trip to the continent, in 1814, was a second elopement. Like Harriet, Mary was only sixteen when she ran away with the poet. By 1816, the year after Shelley had received a substantial inheritance from his grandfather, his circle had expanded to include Mary's step-sister Claire Clairmont, Thomas Love Peacock, and Lord Byron, whom the extended family met in Geneva.

Yet new-found financial security cannot have blinded the poet to the risks of continued activism. Mary Shelley's *annus mirabilis* – 1817, the first of her married life and the year in which she published *Frankenstein* – saw the suspension of Habeas Corpus, the right to demand a fair trial. Writers opposed to the government could now be summarily imprisoned. Across the Channel, the apotheosis of Napoleon was followed by the battle of Waterloo; while in Britain the dual upheavals of the agricultural and industrial revolutions had created a new class of urban poor, rendered increasingly desperate by Corn Laws which kept the price of that staple artificially high. Their escalating protests would culminate, by 1820, in the Cato Street Conspiracy, the unsuccessful plot to murder the British Cabinet which was conceived at least partly in response to the Peterloo Massacre. That atrocity, when cavalry charged a peaceful meeting in St Peter's Field, Manchester, killing fifteen people and injuring hundreds, prompted Shelley's long protest poem, *The Mask of Anarchy,* which adopted the ballad form often associated with political pamphleteers.

Unsurprisingly perhaps, in 1818 the Shelleys settled permanently in Italy. It was now that Percy Bysshe would write most of his mature poetry. The move seems to have freed him from a sense of obligation to direct political engagement, though his literary relationships intensified. As well as developing friendships with Byron, Leigh Hunt, Thomas Medwin, the autobiographer and adventurer Edward Trelawny, and Edward and Jane Williams, in 1820 he invited John Keats, ill with TB, to come and live with him in Italy. Terms with senior poets, however, could be strained. *Peter Bell the Third*, Shelley's skit portraying Wordsworth's inability to resist the seductions of the literary establishment, which not surprisingly the publisher failed to issue, is the more cruel for being so astute.

Nevertheless, the first Romantic generation's strenuous self-involvement, Coleridge's psychedelia and Wordsworth's diarism alike, was what allowed the lighter, arguably more persuasive lyric touch of Keats, Shelley's expanded lyric, and Byron's applied Romanticism to emerge. Alongside the earlier, sometimes rather stagey self-invention, a more internalised consciousness makes itself heard in the work of Shelley's maturity. For example, 1816's 'Mont Blanc', published as part of Mary and Percy Bysshe's account of their first European trip, shifts his preoccupation with action and consequence from a simple matter of morality to an existential question about how the world works. Thinking about human nature in terms of its actions seems, in other words, to have led him to think about the actions of the natural world. Living beyond the jurisdiction of the Church and after the Death of God, the young radical needed to make sense of these. His original subtitle, 'Lines written in the Vale of Chamouni', explicitly alluded to Coleridge's 1802 'Hymn before Sunrise, in the Vale of Chamouni'. But he replaces Coleridge's transcendence with the action of meaning in the here-and-now. The Alp doesn't help Shelley *think about* power, it *is* powerful: 'Mont Blanc yet gleams on high: the power is there'.

The opening metaphors of 'Ode to the West Wind', written five years later, express a closely related paradox. While a wind may be invisible, its actions in and on the world are palpable. It is present *through or as* its agency:

O wild West Wind, thou breath of Autumn's being,
Thou, from whose unseen presence the leaves dead
Are driven, like ghosts from an enchanter fleeing,

[...]   O thou,
Who chariotest to their dark wintry bed

The wingéd seeds, [...]

This fusion of power and intention seems not a million miles from conventional nineteenth-century ideas of God. It also offered Shelley a model for the way human consciousness, including the consciousness the poem expresses, might operate in the world. The contemporary revolution in experimental science – this was the era of Edward Jenner and James Watt – would have made it possible for Shelley to conceptualise the human 'thinking thing' as both brain and mind. Moreover, the ideas of John Locke and David Hume had influenced the young writer at Oxford; Mary Shelley claimed that George Berkeley's immaterialism was formative, too. These eighteenth-century natural philosophers queried the qualitative distinction between, for example, the material actions of light on the eye and the immaterial understanding those actions could produce. In 'Hymn to Intellectual Beauty', *de facto* a companion piece to 'Mont Blanc', thought is a non-abstract, palpable, entity that operates in the world in ways analogous to natural forces. 'Mont Blanc' itself uses ruggedly uneven 'spontaneous' rhyme pattern and line-length to mimic 'natural' forcefulness.

Mimesis is important in several other later poems. Shelley uses it to demonstrate, rather than describe, rapture. Instead of informing us about this experience, the poetry demands that the reader him or herself be 'carried away'. It's the opposite of Wordsworth's 'emotion recollected in tranquility', and places Shelley in a radical counter-tradition to realist, descriptive or even confessional poetry. That counter-tradition runs from Shelley's German Romantic near-contemporary Friedrich Hölderlin, celebrant of the 'on-rushing word', to – in the twentieth century – Virginia Woolf's use of stream of consciousness, the American Beat poets, or even what French philosopher Hélène Cixous calls a 'strategy of velocity'. Each of these writers piles up so many words that they seem to tumble down the page, creating an effect of speed. They may do so for a number of reasons: to make the reader hear an idea afresh, to accommodate wide-ranging material, to create richness, or to recreate the actual movement of experience. All these impulses form part of Shelley's work.

Of course, poems don't have musical tempo markings; writing which depended upon literal reading speed would be more performance script than poem. But poets and prose writers working in this tradition do score a longer line and so a different diction than that of, for example, the ballad:

> The joy, the triumph, the delight, the madness!
> The boundless, overflowing, bursting gladness,
> The vaporous exultation not to be confined!
> Ha! Ha! the animation of delight
> Which wraps me, like an atmosphere of light,
> And bears me as a cloud is borne by its own wind.
>
> ('Earth', in *Prometheus Unbound* iv)

Helter-skelter versification like this requires our participation: to speak these lines is to become literally breathless. Just as, in the 'Letter to Maria Gisborne', the reader's viewpoint is used as part of the poem's thematic material, here the *act* of reading is inseparable from the way the prosody works.

Possibly, such demands on our own resources and commitment intervene between a contemporary readership and Robert Browning's star-struck exclamation, in 'Memorabilia', 'Ah, did you once see Shelley plain?' We can feel overwhelmed by the sense of willy-nilly complicity, as well as by the way polemic raises the stakes for whatever it is we've been made complicit in. Also overwhelming is the sheer range of things going on. Shelley is an elegist, a narrative poet, a poet of ideas, and a rhapsode; occasionally all at the same time, as in *Adonais*, his book-length elegy for Keats:

> His head was bound with pansies overblown,
> And faded violets, white, and pied, and blue;
> And a light spear topped a cypress cone,
> Round whose rude shaft dark ivy-tresses grew
> Yet dripping with the forest's noonday dew,

Vibrated, as the ever-beating heart
Shook the weak hand that grasped it; of that crew
He came the last, neglected and apart;
A herd-abandoned deer struck by the hunter's dart.

He also has a tendency to synthesise. *Adonais* not only pays specific homage, in its choice of stanza form, to *Asphodel,* Edmund Spenser's elegy for Sir Philip Sidney, but imports into that pastoral elegy tradition a Fisher King myth with debts to both the Greek myth of Adonis and the Hebrew word (and idea) *Adonai* ('Lord').

Throughout his work, lyrics both short and long move to a characteristic music of threes, whether the three-step thumbnail in 'Ode to a Skylark':

Sound of vernal showers
    On the twinkling grass,
Rain-awakened flowers [. . .]

or the trio of metaphors which mark the end of a romantic triangle (in the poem Mary Shelley titled 'To Edward Williams'):

The serpent is shut out from Paradise.
    The wounded deer must seek the herb no more
        In which its heart-cure lies:
    The widowed dove must cease to haunt a bower
Like that from which its mate with feignèd sighs
        Fled in the April hour.

Moreover, Shelley uses synthesis to recast both ideas and conclusions. Written in the *terza rima* of Dante's *Divine Comedy,* his final long poem *The Triumph of Life* – which was left unfinished at his death – replaces Virgil's poetic-guide to an afterlife with Rousseau as philosopher-guide to this life. In this secular retort to the Christian system, Rousseau's shade warns the narrator against 'the mighty Phantoms of an elder day', for 'all things are transfigured, except Love' by the difficulties of life – but also by our incomprehension.

Shelley's faith in self-reliance had arguably fatal consequences. In the summer of 1822, he and Edward Williams took the newly-built *Don Juan* from Lerici to Leghorn, to meet Leigh Hunt and help him and his family settle into their new home in Pisa. Shelley had proposed that Leigh Hunt and he should collaborate with Byron on a literary review which they planned to call *The Liberal*. On their return journey, across what is now called the Gulf of Poets, the friends sailed into a summer storm and were drowned. It's a well-rehearsed irony that Shelley left the draft of *The Triumph of Life* unfinished before he had answered the question, 'Then, what is Life?'

NOTE ON THE TEXT

Shelley was attracted to longer forms, including the verse-drama, a form which is necessarily compromised on the page. In making this selection I've wanted to retain some sense of that scale, by printing significant longer poems – *The Mask of Anarchy*, *Letter to Maria Gisborne*, *Adonais* and *The Triumph of Life* – whole. Where space has forced a choice between poems of scholarly interest and those of more direct appeal to today's readers, I've chosen the latter. Students and scholars will be well-served by Donald H. Reiman and Neil Fraistat's existing Norton *Critical Edition* as well as their *Complete* Norton edition, and Kelvin Everest's for Pearson Longman, in preparation.

Since much of Shelley's work was unpublished in his lifetime, these poems are arranged in our best current guess at order of completion. However, this lack of consistent publication history also means final versions of each poem may be obscure and contested. The notebooks are chaotic with revisions; in particular, they're unsystematically punctuated. Even where he did see poems published, Shelley was often dissatisfied. As he wrote to the publisher of *Prometheus Unbound*, 'It is to be regretted that the errors of the press are so numerous.' We have his corrections to that edition, but elsewhere even his fair copies are not always sole or final versions. In her 1824 edition, *Posthumous Poems*, for example, Mary Shelley published the material that would become 'To Jane: The Invitation' and 'To Jane: The Recollection' as a single early draft, called 'The Pine Forest of the Cascine near Pisa'. It seems she only became aware of these loving addresses to another woman as two distinct and fully-worked poems by the time of *The Poetical Works of P.B.S.*, in 1839. Specialist scholars are still establishing Shelleyan final versions for each poem, and it would be foolish for this edition to try to outstrip their distinguished forensic acuity. I've therefore based these texts on the standard Thomas Hutchinson edition of 1929, although in 'The Triumph of Life' I have followed contemporary consensus in stripping out Mary Shelley's amendations. But, since my intention is above all to produce a readable Shelley, I've stripped out some of Hutchinson's subsequent punctuations, silently corrected archaic or unconventional spellings, and standardised capitalisation within each poem.

PERCY BYSSHE SHELLEY

from Queen Mab

[1, lines 130–56]

      Sudden arose
    Ianthe's Soul; it stood
All beautiful in naked purity,
The perfect semblance of its bodily frame.
Instinct with inexpressible beauty and grace,
    Each stain of earthliness
  Had passed away, it reassumed
  Its native dignity, and stood
    Immortal amid ruin.

  Upon the couch the body lay
  Wrapped in the depth of slumber:
Its features were fixed and meaningless,
  Yet animal life was there,
And every organ yet performed
Its natural functions: 'twas a sight
Of wonder to behold the body and soul.
  The self-same lineaments, the same
  Marks of identity were there:
Yet, oh, how different! One aspires to Heaven,
Pants for its sempiternal heritage,
And ever-changing, ever-rising still,
    Wantons in endless being.
The other, for a time the unwilling sport
Of circumstance and passion, struggles on;
Fleets through its sad duration rapidly:
Then, like a useless and worn-out machine,
    Rots, perishes, and passes.

All things are sold: the very light of Heaven
Is venal; earth's unsparing gifts of love,
The smallest and most despicable things
That lurk in the abysses of the deep,
All objects of our life, even life itself,
And the poor pittance which the laws allow
Of liberty, the fellowship of man,
Those duties which his heart of human love
Should urge him to perform instinctively,
Are bought and sold as in a public mart
Of undisguising selfishness, that sets
On each its price, the stamp-mark of her reign.
Even love is sold; the solace of all woe
Is turned to deadliest agony, old age
Shivers in selfish beauty's loathing arms,
And youth's corrupted impulses prepare
A life of horror from the blighting bane
Of commerce; whilst the pestilence that springs
From unenjoying sensualism, has filled
All human life with hydra-headed woes.

Mutability

We are as clouds that veil the midnight moon;
  How restlessly they speed, and gleam, and quiver,
Streaking the darkness radiantly!—yet soon
  Night closes round, and they are lost for ever:

Or like forgotten lyres, whose dissonant strings
  Give various response to each varying blast,
To whose frail frame no second motion brings
  One mood or modulation like the last.

We rest.—A dream has power to poison sleep;
  We rise.—One wandering thought pollutes the day;
We feel, conceive or reason, laugh or weep;
  Embrace fond foe, or cast our cares away:

It is the same!—For, be it joy or sorrow,
  The path of its departure still is free:
Man's yesterday may ne'er be like his morrow;
  Nought may endure but Mutability.

To Wordsworth

Poet of Nature, thou hast wept to know
That things depart which never may return:
Childhood and youth, friendship and love's first glow,
Have fled like sweet dreams, leaving thee to mourn.
These common woes I feel. One loss is mine
Which thou too feel'st, yet I alone deplore.
Thou wert as a lone star, whose light did shine
On some frail bark in winter's midnight roar:
Thou hast like to a rock-built refuge stood
Above the blind and battling multitude:
In honoured poverty thy voice did weave
Songs consecrate to truth and liberty,—
Deserting these, thou leavest me to grieve,
Thus having been, that thou shouldst cease to be.

Hymn to Intellectual Beauty

I

The awful shadow of some unseen Power
   Floats through unseen among us,—visiting
   This various world with as inconstant wing
As summer winds that creep from flower to flower,—
Like moonbeams that behind some piny mountain shower,
     It visits with inconstant glance
     Each human heart and countenance;
Like hues and harmonies of evening,—
     Like clouds in starlight widely spread,—
     Like memory of music fled,—
     Like aught that for its grace may be
Dear, and yet dearer for its mystery.

II

Spirit of Beauty, that doth consecrate
   With thine own hues all thou dost shine upon
   Of human thought or form,—where art thou gone?
Why dost thou pass away and leave our state,
This dim vast vale of tears, vacant and desolate?
     Ask why the sunlight not for ever
     Weaves rainbows o'er yon mountain-river,
Why aught should fail and fade that once is shown,
     Why fear and dream and death and birth
     Cast on the daylight of this earth
     Such gloom,—why man has such a scope
For love and hate, despondency and hope?

III

No voice from some sublimer world hath ever
   To sage or poet these responses given—
   Therefore the names of Demon, Ghost, and Heaven,
Remain the records of their vain endeavour,
Frail spells—whose uttered charm might not avail to sever,

7

From all we hear and all we see,
Doubt, chance, and mutability.
Thy light alone—like mist o'er mountains driven,
Or music by the night-wind sent
Through strings of some still instrument,
Or moonlight on a midnight stream,
Gives grace and truth to life's unquiet dream.

IV

Love, Hope, and Self-esteem, like clouds depart
And come, for some uncertain moments lent.
Man were immortal, and omnipotent,
Didst thou, unknown and awful as thou art,
Keep with thy glorious train firm state within his heart.
Thou messenger of sympathies,
That wax and wane in lovers' eyes—
Thou—that to human thought are nourishment,
Like darkness to a dying flame!
Depart not as thy shadow came,
Depart not—lest the grave should be,
Like life and fear, a dark reality.

V

While yet a boy I sought for ghosts, and sped
Through many a listening chamber, cave and ruin,
And starlight wood, with fearful steps pursuing
Hopes of high talk with the departed dead.
I called on poisonous names with which our youth is fed;
I was not heard—I saw them not—
When musing deeply on the lot
Of life, at that sweet time when winds are wooing
All vital things that wake to bring
News of buds and blossoming,—
Sudden, thy shadow fell on me;
I shrieked, and clasped my hands in ecstasy!

VI

I vowed that I would dedicate my powers
  To thee and thine—have I not kept the vow?
  With beating heart and streaming eyes, even now
I call the phantoms of a thousand hours
Each from his voiceless grave: they have in visioned bowers
    Of studious zeal or love's delight
    Outwatched with me the envious night—
They know that never joy illumed my brow
    Unlinked with hope that thou wouldst free
    This world from its dark slavery,
    That thou—O awful Loveliness,
Wouldst give whate'er these words cannot express.

VII

The day becomes more solemn and serene
  When noon is past—there is a harmony
  In autumn, and a lustre in its sky,
Which through the summer is not heard or seen,
As if it could not be, as if it had not been!
    Thus let thy power, which like the truth
    Of nature on my passive youth
  Descended, to my onward life supply
    Its calm—to one who worships thee,
    And every form containing thee,
    Whom, Spirit fair, thy spells did bind
To fear himself, and love all human kind.

Mont Blanc
Lines written in the Vale of Chamouni

I

The everlasting universe of things
Flows through the mind, and rolls its rapid waves,
Now dark—now glittering—now reflecting gloom—
Now lending splendour, where from secret springs
The source of human thought its tribute brings
Of waters,—with a sound but half its own,
Such as a feeble brook will oft assume
In the wild woods, among the mountains lone,
Where waterfalls around it leap for ever,
Where woods and winds contend, and a vast river
Over its rocks ceaselessly bursts and raves.

II

Thus thou, Ravine of Arve—dark, deep Ravine—
Thou many-coloured, many-voicèd vale,
Over whose pines, and crags, and caverns sail
Fast cloud shadows and sunbeams: awful scene,
Where Power in likeness of the Arve comes down
From the ice-gulfs that gird his secret throne,
Bursting through these dark mountains like the flame
Of lightning through the tempest;—thou dost lie,
Thy giant brood of pines around thee clinging,
Children of elder time, in whose devotion
The chainless winds still come and ever came
To drink their odours, and their mighty swinging
To hear—an old and solemn harmony;
Thine earthly rainbows stretched across the sweep
Of the ethereal waterfall, whose veil
Robes some unsculptured image; the strange sleep
Which when the voices of the desert fail
Wraps all in its own deep eternity;—

Thy caverns echoing to the Arve's commotion,
A loud, lone sound no other sound can tame;
Thou art pervaded with that ceaseless motion,
Thou art the path of that unresting sound—
Dizzy Ravine! and when I gaze on thee
I seem as in a trance sublime and strange
To muse on my own separate fantasy,
My own, my human mind, which passively
Now renders and receives fast influencings,
Holding an unremitting interchange
With the clear universe of things around;
One legion of wild thoughts, whose wandering wings
Now float above thy darkness, and now rest
Where that or thou art no unbidden guest,
In the still cave of the witch Poesy,
Seeking among the shadows that pass by
Ghosts of all things that are, some shade of thee,
Some phantom, some faint image; till the breast
From which they fled recalls them, thou art there!

III

Some say that gleams of a remoter world
Visit the soul in sleep,—that death is slumber,
And that its shapes the busy thoughts outnumber
Of those who wake and live.—I look on high;
Has some unknown omnipotence unfurled
The veil of life and death? or do I lie
In dream, and does the mightier world of sleep
Spread far and round and inaccessibly
Its circles? For the very spirit fails,
Driven like a homeless cloud from steep to steep
That vanishes among the viewless gales!
Far, far above, piercing the infinite sky,
Mont Blanc appears,—still, snowy and serene—
Its subject mountains their unearthly forms
Pile around it, ice and rock; broad vales between

Of frozen floods, unfathomable deeps,
Blue as the overhanging heaven, that spread
And wind among the accumulated steeps;
A desert peopled by the storms alone,
Save when the eagle brings some hunter's bone,
And the wolf tracks her there—how hideously
Its shapes are heaped around! rude, bare, and high,
Ghastly, and scarred, and riven.—Is this the scene
Where the old Earthquake-daemon taught her young
Ruin? Were these their toys? or did a sea
Of fire envelop once this silent snow?
None can reply—all seems eternal now.
The wilderness has a mysterious tongue
Which teaches awful doubt, or faith so mild,
So solemn, so serene, that man may be
But for such faith with nature reconciled;
Thou hast a voice, great Mountain, to repeal
Large codes of fraud and woe; not understood
By all, but which the wise, and great, and good
Interpret, or make felt, or deeply feel.

IV

The fields, the lakes, the forests, and the streams,
Ocean, and all the living things that dwell
Within the daedal earth; lightning, and rain,
Earthquake, and fiery flood, and hurricane,
The torpor of the year when feeble dreams
Visit the hidden buds, or dreamless sleep
Holds every future leaf and flower;—the bound
With which from that detested trance they leap;
The works and ways of man, their death and birth,
And that of him and all that his may be;
All things that move and breathe with toil and sound
Are born and die; revolve, subside, and swell.
Power dwells apart in its tranquility,
Remote, serene, and inaccessible:

And *this*, the naked countenance of earth,
On which I gaze, even these primeval mountains
Teach the adverting mind. The glaciers creep
Like snakes that watch their prey, from their far fountains,
Slow rolling on; there, many a precipice,
Frost and the Sun in scorn of mortal power
Have piled: dome, pyramid, and pinnacle,
A city of death, distinct with many a tower
And wall impregnable of beaming ice.
Yet not a city, but a flood of ruin
Is there, that from the boundaries of the sky
Rolls its perpetual stream; vast pines are strewing
Its destined path, or in the mangled soil
Branchless and shattered stand; the rocks, drawn down
From yon remotest waste, have overthrown
The limits of the dead and living world,
Never to be reclaimed. The dwelling-place
Of insects, beasts, and birds, becomes its spoil
Their food and their retreat for ever gone,
So much of life and joy is lost. The race
Of man flies far in dread; his work and dwelling
Vanish, like smoke before the tempest's stream,
And their place is not known. Below, vast caves
Shine in the rushing torrents' restless gleam,
Which from those secret chasms in tumult welling
Meet in the vale, and one majestic River,
The breath and blood of distant lands, for ever
Rolls its loud waters to the ocean-waves,
Breathes its swift vapours to the circling air.

v

Mont Blanc yet gleams on high:—the power is there,
The still and solemn power of many sights,
And many sounds, and much of life and death.
In the calm darkness of the moonless nights,
In the lone glare of day, the snows descend

Upon that Mountain; none beholds them there,
Nor when the flakes burn in the sinking sun,
Or the star-beams dart through them:—Winds contend
Silently there, and heap the snow with breath
Rapid and strong, but silently! Its home
The voiceless lightning in these solitudes
Keeps innocently, and like vapour broods
Over the snow. The secret Strength of things
Which governs thought, and to the infinite dome
Of Heaven is as a law, inhabits thee!
And what were thou, and earth, and stars, and sea,
If to the human mind's imaginings
Silence and solitude were vacancy?

Ozymandias

I met a traveller from an antique land
Who said: 'Two vast and trunkless legs of stone
Stand in the desert . . . Near them, on the sand,
Half sunk, a shattered visage lies, whose frown,
And wrinkled lip, and sneer of cold command,
Tell that its sculptor well those passions read
Which yet survive, stamped on these lifeless things,
The hand that mocked them, and the heart that fed;
And on the pedestal these words appear:
"My name is Ozymandias, king of kings:
Look on my works, ye Mighty, and despair!"
Nothing beside remains. Round the decay
Of that colossal wreck, boundless and bare
The lone and level sands stretch far away.'

Stanzas written in Dejection, near Naples

The sun is warm, the sky is clear,
    The waves are dancing fast and bright,
Blue isles and snowy mountains wear
    The purple noon's transparent might,
    The breath of the moist earth is light
Around its unexpanded buds;
    Like many a voice of one delight,
The winds, the birds, the ocean-floods,
The City's voice itself is soft, like Solitude's.

I see the deep's untrampled floor
    With green and purple seaweeds strown;
I see the waves upon the shore
    Like light dissolved in star-showers, thrown:
    I sit upon the sands alone,—
The lightning of the noontide ocean
    Is flashing round me, and a tone
Arises from its measured motion,
How sweet! did any heart now share in my emotion.

Alas! I have nor hope nor health,
    Nor peace within nor calm around,
Nor that content surpassing wealth
    The sage in meditation found,
    And walked with inward glory crowned—
Nor fame, nor power, nor love, nor leisure.
    Others I see whom these surround—
Smiling they live, and call life pleasure;—
To me that cup has been dealt in another measure.

Yet now despair itself is mild,
   Even as the winds and waters are;
I could lie down like a tired child,
   And weep away the life of care
   Which I have borne and yet must bear,
Till death like sleep might steal on me,
   And I might feel in the warm air
My cheek grow cold, and hear the sea
Breathe o'er my dying brain its last monotony.

Some might lament that I were cold,
   As I, when this sweet day is gone,
Which my lost heart, too soon grown old,
   Insults with this untimely moan;
   They might lament—for I am one
Whom men love not,—and yet regret,
   Unlike this day, which, when the sun
Shall on its stainless glory set,
Will linger, though enjoyed, like joy in memory yet.

Sonnet

Lift not the painted veil which those who live
Call Life: though unreal shapes be pictured there,
And it but mimic all we would believe
With colours idly spread,—behind, lurk Fear
And Hope, twin Destinies; who ever weave
Their shadows, o'er the chasm, sightless and drear.
I knew one who had lifted it—he sought,
For his lost heart was tender, things to love,
But found them not, alas! nor was there aught
The world contains, the which he could approve.
Through the unheeding many he did move,
A splendour among shadows, a bright blot
Upon this gloomy scene, a Spirit that strove
For truth, and like the Preacher found it not.

from Julian and Maddalo

[Lines 1–140]

I rode one evening with Count Maddalo
Upon the bank of land which breaks the flow
Of Adria towards Venice: a bare strand
Of hillocks, heaped from ever-shifting sand,
Matted with thistles and amphibious weeds,
Such as from earth's embrace the salt ooze breeds,
Is this; an uninhabited sea-side
Which the lone fisher, when his nets are dried,
Abandons; and no other object breaks
The waste, but one dwarf tree and some few stakes
Broken and unrepaired, and the tide makes
A narrow space of level sand thereon,
Where 'twas our wont to ride while day went down.
This ride was my delight. I love all waste
And solitary places; where we taste
The pleasure of believing what we see
Is boundless, as we wish our souls to be:
And such was this wide ocean, and this shore
More barren than its billows; and yet more
Than all, with a remembered friend I love
To ride as then I rode;—for the winds drove
The living spray along the sunny air
Into our faces; the blue heavens were bare,
Stripped to their depths by the awakening North;
And, from the waves, sound like delight broke forth
Harmonizing with solitude, and sent
Into our hearts aëreal merriment.
So, as we rode, we talked; and the swift thought,
Winging itself with laughter, lingered not,
But flew from brain to brain,—such glee was ours,

Charged with light memories of remembered hours,
None slow enough for sadness: till we came
Homeward, which always makes the spirit tame.
This day had been cheerful but cold, and now
The sun was sinking, and the wind also.
Our talk grew somewhat serious, as may be
Talk interrupted with such raillery
As mocks itself, because it cannot scorn
The thoughts it would extinguish:—'twas forlorn,
Yet pleasing, such as once, so poets tell,
The devils held within the dales of Hell
Concerning God, freewill and destiny:
Of all that earth has been or yet may be,
All that vain men imagine or believe,
Or hope can paint or suffering may achieve,
We descanted, and I (for ever still
Is it not wise to make the best of ill?)
Argued against despondency, but pride
Made my companion take the darker side.
The sense that he was greater than his kind
Had struck, methinks, his eagle spirit blind
By gazing on its own exceeding light.
Meanwhile the sun paused ere it should alight,
Over the horizon of the mountains;—Oh
How beautiful is sunset, when the glow
Of Heaven descends upon a land like thee,
Thou Paradise of exiles, Italy!
Thy mountains, seas and vineyards and the towers
Of cities they encircle!—it was ours
To stand on thee, beholding it: and then
Just where we had dismounted the Count's men
Were waiting for us with the gondola.—
As those who pause on some delightful way
Though bent on pleasant pilgrimage, we stood
Looking upon the evening and the flood
Which lay between the city and the shore,
Paved with the image of the sky ... the hoar

And aëry Alps towards the North appeared
Through mist, an heaven-sustaining bulwark reared
Between the East and West; and half the sky
Was roofed with clouds of rich emblazonry
Dark purple at the zenith, which still grew
Down the steep West into a wondrous hue
Brighter than burning gold, even to the rent
Where the swift sun yet paused in his descent
Among the many-folded hills: they were
Those famous Euganean hills, which bear
As seen from Lido through the harbour piles
The likeness of a clump of peakèd isles—
And then—as if the Earth and Sea had been
Dissolved into one lake of fire, were seen
Those mountains towering as from waves of flame
Around the vaporous sun, from which there came
The inmost purple spirit of light, and made
Their very peaks transparent. 'Ere it fade,'
Said my companion, 'I will show you soon
A better station'—so, o'er the lagoon
We glided; and from that funereal bark
I leaned, and saw the city, and could mark
How from their many isles in evening's gleam
Its temples and its palaces did seem
Like fabrics of enchantment piled to Heaven.
I was about to speak, when—'We are even
Now at the point I meant,' said Maddalo
And bade the gondolieri cease to row.
'Look, Julian, on the West, and listen well
If you hear not a deep and heavy bell.'
I looked, and saw between us and the sun
A building on an island; such a one
As age to age might add, for uses vile,
A windowless, deformed and dreary pile;
And on the top an open tower, where hung
A bell, which in the radiance swayed and swung;
We could just hear its hoarse and iron tongue:

The broad sun sunk behind it, and it tolled
In strong and black relief—'What we behold
Shall be the madhouse and its belfry tower,'
Said Maddalo, 'and ever at this hour
Those who may cross the water, hear that bell
Which calls the maniacs each one from his cell
To vespers.'—'As much skill as need to pray
In thanks or hope for their dark lot have they
To their stern maker,' I replied. 'O ho!
You talk as in years past,' said Maddalo.
''Tis strange men change not. You were ever still
Among Christ's flock a perilous infidel,
A wolf for the meek lambs—if you can't swim
Beware of Providence.' I looked on him,
But the gay smile had faded in his eye,
'And such,'—he cried, 'is our mortality,
And this must be the emblem and the sign
Of what should be eternal and divine!—
And like that black and dreary bell, the soul,
Hung in a heaven-illumined tower, must toll
Our thoughts and our desires to meet below
Round the rent heart and pray—as madmen do
For what? they know not,—till the night of death
As sunset that strange vision, severeth
Our memory from itself, and us from all
We sought and yet were baffled.' I recall
The sense of what he said, although I mar
The force of his expressions. The broad star
Of day meanwhile had sunk behind the hill,
And the black bell became invisible
And the red tower looked gray, and all between
The churches, ships and palaces were seen
Huddled in gloom;—into the purple sea
The orange hues of heaven sunk silently.
We hardly spoke, and soon the gondola
Conveyed me to my lodgings by the way.

The Mask of Anarchy
Written on the occasion of the massacre at Manchester

As I lay asleep in Italy
There came a voice from over the Sea,
And with great power it forth led me
To walk in the visions of Poesy.

I met Murder on the way—
He had a mask like Castlereagh—
Very smooth he looked, yet grim;
Seven blood-hounds followed him:

All were fat; and well they might
Be in admirable plight,
For one by one, and two by two,
He tossed them human hearts to chew
Which from his wide cloak he drew.

Next came Fraud, and he had on,
Like Eldon, an ermined gown;
His big tears, for he wept well,
Turned to mill-stones as they fell.

And the little children, who
Round his feet played to and fro,
Thinking every tear a gem,
Had their brains knocked out by them.

Clothed with the Bible, as with light,
And the shadows of the night,
Like Sidmouth, next, Hypocrisy
On a crocodile rode by.

And many more Destructions played
In this ghastly masquerade,
All disguised, even to the eyes,
Like Bishops, lawyers, peers, or spies.

Last came Anarchy: he rode
On a white horse, splashed with blood;
He was pale even to the lips,
Like Death in the Apocalypse.

And he wore a kingly crown;
And in his grasp a sceptre shone;
On his brow this mark I saw—
'I am God, and King, and Law!'

With a pace stately and fast,
Over English land he passed,
Trampling to a mire of blood
The adoring multitude.

And a mighty troop around,
With their trampling shook the ground,
Waving each a bloody sword,
For the service of their Lord.

And with glorious triumph, they
Rode through England proud and gay,
Drunk as with intoxication
Of the wine of desolation.

O'er fields and towns, from sea to sea,
Passed the Pageant swift and free,
Tearing up, and trampling down;
Till they came to London town.

And each dweller, panic-stricken,
Felt his heart with terror sicken
Hearing the tempestuous cry
Of the triumph of Anarchy.

For with pomp to meet him came,
Clothed in arms like blood and flame,
The hired murderers, who did sing
'Thou art God, and Law, and King.

'We have waited, weak and lone
For thy coming, Mighty One!
Our purses are empty, our swords are cold,
Give us glory, and blood, and gold.'

Lawyers and priests, a motley crowd,
To the earth their pale brows bowed;
Like a bad prayer not over loud,
Whispering—'Thou art Law and God.'—

Then all cried with one accord,
'Thou art King, and God and Lord;
Anarchy, to thee we bow,
Be thy name made holy now!'

And Anarchy, the Skeleton,
Bowed and grinned to every one,
As well as if his education
Had cost ten millions to the nation.

For he knew the Palaces
Of our Kings were nightly his;
His the sceptre, crown, and globe,
And the gold-inwoven robe.

So he sent his slaves before
To seize upon the Bank and Tower,
And was proceeding with intent
To meet his pensioned Parliament

When one fled past, a maniac maid,
And her name was Hope, she said:
But she looked more like Despair,
And she cried out in the air:

'My father Time is weak and gray
With waiting for a better day;
See how idiot-like he stands,
Fumbling with his palsied hands!

He has had child after child,
And the dust of death is piled
Over every one but me—
Misery, oh, Misery!'

Then she lay down in the street,
Right before the horses' feet,
Expecting, with a patient eye,
Murder, Fraud, and Anarchy.

When between her and her foes
A mist, a light, an image rose,
Small at first, and weak, and frail
Like the vapour of a vale:

Till as clouds grow on the blast,
Like tower-crowned giants striding fast,
And glare with lightnings as they fly,
And speak in thunder to the sky,

It grew—a Shape arrayed in mail
Brighter than the viper's scale,
And upborne on wings whose grain
Was as the light of sunny rain.

On its helm, seen far away,
A planet, like the Morning's, lay;
And those plumes its light rained through
Like a shower of crimson dew.

With step as soft as wind it passed
O'er the heads of men—so fast
That they knew the presence there,
And looked,—and all was empty air.

As flowers beneath May's footstep waken
As stars from Night's loose hair are shaken
As waves arise when loud winds call
Thoughts sprung where'er that step did fall.

And the prostrate multitude
Looked—and ankle-deep in blood,
Hope, that maiden most serene,
Was walking with a quiet mien:

And Anarchy, the ghastly birth,
Lay dead earth upon the earth,
The Horse of Death tameless as wind
Fled, and with his hoofs did grind
To dust the murderers thronged behind.

A rushing light of clouds and splendour,
A sense awakening and yet tender
Was heard and felt—and at its close
These words of joy and fear arose

As if their own indignant Earth
Which gave the sons of England birth
Had felt their blood upon her brow,
And shuddering with a mother's throe

Had turnèd every drop of blood
By which her face had been bedewed
To an accent unwithstood,—
As if her heart had cried aloud:

'Men of England, heirs of Glory,
Heroes of unwritten story,
Nurslings of one mighty Mother,
Hopes of her, and one another;

'Rise like Lions after slumber
In unvanquishable number
Shake your chains to earth like dew
Which in sleep had fallen on you—
Ye are many—they are few.

'What is Freedom?—ye can tell
That which slavery is, too well—
For its very name has grown
To an echo of your own.

''Tis to work and have such pay
As just keeps life from day to day
In your limbs, as in a cell
For the tyrants' use to dwell

'So that ye for them are made
Loom, and plough, and sword, and spade,
With or without your own will bent
To their defence and nourishment.

''Tis to see your children weak
With their mothers pine and peak,
When the winter winds are bleak,—
They are dying whilst I speak.

''Tis to hunger for such diet
As the rich man in his riot
Casts to the fat dogs that lie
Surfeiting beneath his eye;

''Tis to let the Ghost of Gold
Take from Toil a thousandfold
More that e'er its substance could
In the tyrannies of old.

'Paper coin—that forgery
Of the title-deeds, which ye
Hold to something of the worth
Of the inheritance of Earth.

''Tis to be a slave in soul
And to hold no strong control
Over your own wills, but be
All that others make of ye.

'And at length when ye complain
With a murmur weak and vain
'Tis to see the Tyrant's crew
Ride over your wives and you—
Blood is on the grass like dew.

'Then it is to feel revenge
Fiercely thirsting to exchange
Blood for blood—and wrong for wrong—
Do not thus when ye are strong.

'Birds find rest, in narrow nest
When weary of their wingèd quest;
Beasts find fare, in woody lair
When storm and snow are in the air.

'Asses, swine, have litter spread
And with fitting food are fed;
All things have a home but one—
Thou, Oh, Englishman, hast none!

'This is Slavery—savage men
Or wild beasts within a den
Would endure not as ye do—
But such ills they never knew.

'What art thou Freedom? O! could slaves
Answer from their living graves
This demand—tyrants would flee
Like a dream's dim imagery:

'Thou art not, as impostors say,
A shadow soon to pass away,
A superstition, and a name
Echoing from the cave of Fame.

'For the labourer thou art bread,
And a comely table spread
From his daily labour come
To a neat and happy home.

'Thou art clothes, and fire, and food
For the trampled multitude—
No—in countries that are free
Such starvation cannot be
As in England now we see.

'To the rich thou art a check,
When his foot is on the neck
Of his victim, thou dost make
That he treads upon a snake.

'Thou art Justice—ne'er for gold
May thy righteous laws be sold
As laws are in England—thou
Shield'st alike the high and low.

'Thou art Wisdom—Freemen never
Dream that God will damn for ever
All who think those things untrue
Of which Priests make such ado.

'Thou art Peace—never by thee
Would blood and treasure wasted be
As tyrants wasted them, when all
Leagued to quench thy flame in Gaul.

'What if English toil and blood
Was poured forth, even as a flood?
It availed, Oh, Liberty,
To dim, but not extinguish thee.

'Thou art Love—the rich have kissed
Thy feet, and like him following Christ,
Give their substance to the free
And through the rough world follow thee

'Or turn their wealth to arms, and make
War for thy belovèd sake
On wealth, and war, and fraud—whence they
Drew the power which is their prey.

'Science, Poetry, and Thought
Are thy lamps; they make the lot
Of the dwellers in a cot
So serene, they curse it not.

'Spirit, Patience, Gentleness,
All that can adorn and bless
Art thou—let deeds, not words, express
Thine exceeding loveliness.

'Let a great Assembly be
Of the fearless and the free
On some spot of English ground
Where the plains stretch wide around.

'Let the blue sky overhead,
The green earth on which ye tread,
All that must eternal be
Witness the solemnity.

'From the corners uttermost
Of the bounds of English coast;
From every hut, village, and town
Where those who live and suffer moan
For others' misery or their own,

'From the workhouse and the prison
Where pale as corpses newly risen,
Women, children, young and old
Groan for pain, and weep for cold—

'From the haunts of daily life
Where is waged the daily strife
With common wants and common cares
Which sows the human heart with tares—

'Lastly from the palaces
Where the murmur of distress
Echoes, like the distant sound
Of a wind alive around

'Those prison halls of wealth and fashion
Where some few feel such compassion
For those who groan, and toil, and wail
As must make their brethren pale—

'Ye who suffer woes untold,
Or to feel, or to behold
Your lost country bought and sold
With a price of blood and gold—

'Let a vast assembly be,
And with great solemnity
Declare with measured words that ye
Are, as God has made ye, free—

'Be your strong and simple words
Keen to wound as sharpened swords,
And wide as targes let them be,
With their shade to cover ye.

'Let the tyrants pour around
With a quick and startling sound,
Like the loosening of a sea,
Troops of armed emblazonry.

Let the charged artillery drive
Till the dead air seems alive
With the clash of clanging wheels,
And the tramp of horses' heels.

'Let the fixèd bayonet
Gleam with sharp desire to wet
Its bright point in English blood
Looking keen as one for food.

'Let the horsemen's scimitars
Wheel and flash, like sphereless stars
Thirsting to eclipse their burning
In a sea of death and mourning.

'Stand ye calm and resolute,
Like a forest close and mute,
With folded arms and looks which are
Weapons of an unvanquished war,

'And let Panic, who outspeeds
The career of armèd steeds
Pass, a disregarded shade
Through your phalanx undismayed.

'Let the laws of your own land,
Good or ill, between ye stand
Hand to hand, and foot to foot,
Arbiters of the dispute,

'The old laws of England—they
Whose reverend heads with age are gray,
Children of a wiser day;
And whose solemn voice must be
Thine own echo—Liberty!

'On those who first should violate
Such sacred heralds in their state
Rest the blood that must ensue,
And it will not rest on you.

'And if then the tyrants dare
Let them ride among you there,
Slash, and stab, and maim, and hew,—
What they like, that let them do.

'With folded arms and steady eyes,
And little fear, and less surprise
Look upon them as they slay
Till their rage has died away.

'Then they will return with shame
To the place from which they came,
And the blood thus shed will speak
In hot blushes on their cheek.

'Every woman in the land
Will point at them as they stand—
They will hardly dare to greet
Their acquaintance in the street.

'And the bold, true warriors
Who have hugged Danger in wars
Will turn to those who would be free,
Ashamed of such base company.

'And that slaughter to the Nation
Shall steam up like inspiration,
Eloquent, oracular;
A volcano heard afar.

'And these words shall then become
Like Oppression's thundered doom
Ringing through each heart and brain,
Heard again—again—again—

'Rise like Lions after slumber
In unvanquishable number—
Shake your chains to earth like dew
Which in sleep had fallen on you—
Ye are many—they are few.'

Ode to the West Wind

O wild West Wind, thou breath of Autumn's being,
Thou, from whose unseen presence the leaves dead
Are driven, like ghosts from an enchanter fleeing,

Yellow, and black, and pale, and hectic red,
Pestilence-stricken multitudes: O thou,
Who chariotest to their dark wintry bed

The wingéd seeds, where they lie cold and low,
Each like a corpse within its grave, until
Thine azure sister of the Spring shall blow

Her clarion o'er the dreaming earth, and fill
(Driving sweet buds like flocks to feed in air)
With living hues and odors plain and hill:

Wild Spirit, which art moving everywhere;
Destroyer and preserver; hear, oh, hear!

II

Thou on whose stream, 'mid the steep sky's commotion,
Loose clouds like earth's decaying leaves are shed,
Shook from the tangled boughs of Heaven and Ocean,

Angels of rain and lightning: there are spread
On the blue surface of thine aery surge,
Like the bright hair uplifted from the head

Of some fierce Maenad, even from the dim verge
Of the horizon to the zenith's height,
The locks of the approaching storm. Thou dirge

Of the dying year, to which this closing night
Will be the dome of a vast sepulchre,
Vaulted with all thy congregated might

Of vapours, from whose solid atmosphere
Black rain, and fire, and hail will burst: oh, hear!

III

Thou who didst waken from his summer dreams
The blue Mediterranean, where he lay,
Lulled by the coil of his crystalline streams,

Beside a pumice isle in Baiae's bay,
And saw in sleep old palaces and towers
Quivering within the wave's intenser day,

All overgrown with azure moss and flowers
So sweet, the sense faints picturing them! Thou
For whose path the Atlantic's level powers

Cleave themselves into chasms, while far below
The sea-blooms and the oozy woods which wear
The sapless foliage of the ocean, know

Thy voice, and suddenly grow gray with fear,
And tremble and despoil themselves: oh, hear!

IV

If I were a dead leaf thou mightest bear;
If I were a swift cloud to fly with thee;
A wave to pant beneath thy power, and share

The impulse of thy strength, only less free
Than thou, O uncontrollable! If even
I were as in my boyhood, and could be

The comrade of thy wanderings over Heaven,
As then, when to outstrip thy skiey speed
Scarce seemed a vision; I would ne'er have striven

As thus with thee in prayer in my sore need.
Oh, lift me as a wave, a leaf, a cloud!
I fall upon the thorns of life! I bleed!

A heavy weight of hours has chained and bowed
One too like thee: tameless, and swift, and proud.

v

Make me thy lyre, even as the forest is:
What if my leaves are falling like its own!
The tumult of thy mighty harmonies

Will take from both a deep, autumnal tone,
Sweet though in sadness. Be thou, Spirit fierce,
My spirit! Be thou me, impetuous one!

Drive my dead thoughts over the universe
Like withered leaves to quicken a new birth!
And, by the incantation of this verse,

Scatter, as from an unextinguished hearth
Ashes and sparks, my words among mankind!
Be through my lips to unawakened earth

The trumpet of a prophecy! O, Wind,
If Winter comes, can Spring be far behind?

England in 1819

An old, mad, blind, despised, and dying king,—
Princes, the dregs of their dull race, who flow
Through public scorn,—mud from a muddy spring,—
Rulers who neither see, nor feel, nor know,
But leech-like to their fainting country cling,
Till they drop, blind in blood, without a blow,—
A people starved and stabbed in the untilled field,—
An army, which liberticide and prey
Makes as a two-edged sword to all who wield,—
Golden and sanguine laws which tempt and slay;
Religion Christless, Godless—a book sealed;
A Senate,—Time's worst statute unrepealed,—
Are graves, from which a glorious Phantom may
Burst, to illumine our tempestous day.

from Prometheus Unbound

[I, lines 352–409]

MERCURY   Awful Sufferer!
To thee unwilling, most unwillingly
I come, by the great Father's will driven down,
To execute a doom of new revenge.
Alas! I pity thee, and hate myself
That I can do no more: aye from thy sight
Returning, for a season, Heaven seems Hell,
So thy worn form pursues me night and day,
Smiling reproach. Wise art thou, firm and good,
But vainly wouldst stand forth alone in strife
Against the Omnipotent; as yon clear lamps
That measure and divide the weary years
From which there is no refuge, long have taught
And long must teach. Even now thy Torturer arms
With the strange might of unimagined pains
The powers who scheme slow agonies in Hell,
And my commission is to lead them here,
Or what more subtle, foul, or savage fiends
People the abyss, and leave them to their task.
Be it not so! there is a secret known
To thee, and to none else of living things,
Which may transfer the sceptre of wide Heaven,
The fear of which perplexes the Supreme:
Clothe it in words, and bid it clasp his throne
In intercession; bend thy soul in prayer,
And like a suppliant in some gorgeous fane,
Let the will kneel within thy haughty heart:
For benefits and meek submission tame
The fiercest and the mightiest.

Change good to their own nature. I gave all
He has; and in return he chains me here
Years, ages, night and day: whether the Sun
Split my parched skin, or in the moony night
The crystal-wingèd snow cling round my hair:
Whilst my belovèd race is trampled down
By his thought-executing ministers.
Such is the tyrant's recompense: 'tis just:
He who is evil can receive no good;
And for a world bestowed, or a friend lost,
He can feel hate, fear, shame; not gratitude:
He but requites me for his own misdeed.
Kindness to such is keen reproach, which breaks
With bitter stings the light sleep of Revenge.
Submission, thou dost know I cannot try:
For what submission but that fatal word,
The death-seal of mankind's captivity,
Like the Sicilian's hair-suspended sword,
Which trembles o'er his crown, would he accept,
Or could I yield? Which yet I will not yield.
Let others flatter Crime, where it sits throned
In brief Omnipotence: secure are they:
For Justice, when triumphant, will weep down
Pity, not punishment, on her own wrongs,
Too much avenged by those who err. I wait,
Enduring thus, the retributive hour
Which since we spake is even nearer now.
But hark, the hell-hounds clamour: fear delay:
Behold! Heaven lowers under thy Father's frown.

CHORUS OF FURIES   From the ends of the earth, from the
                                        ends of the earth,
    Where the night has its grave and the morning its birth,
                Come, come, come!
    Oh, ye who shake hills with the scream of your mirth,
    When cities sink howling in ruin; and ye
    Who with wingless footsteps trample the sea,
    And close upon Shipwreck and Famine's track,
    Sit chattering with joy on the foodless wreck;
                Come, come, come!
            Leave the bed, low, cold, and red,
            Strewed beneath a nation dead;
            Leave the hatred, as in ashes
                Fire is left for future burning:
            It will burst in bloodier flashes
                When ye stir it, soon returning:
            Leave the self-contempt implanted
            In young spirits, sense-enchanted,
                Misery's yet unkindled fuel:
            Leave Hell's secrets half unchanted
                To the maniac dreamer; cruel
            More than ye can be with hate
                Is he with fear.
                Come, come, come!
    We are steaming up from Hell's wide gate
    And we burthen the blast of the atmosphere,
    But vainly we toil till ye come here.

PANTHEA   I see a mighty darkness
   Filling the seat of power, and rays of gloom
   Dart round, as light from the meridian sun.
   —Ungazed upon and shapeless; neither limb,
   Nor form, nor outline; yet we feel it is
   A living Spirit.
DEMOGORGON   Ask what thou wouldst know.
ASIA What canst thou tell?
DEMOGORGON   All things thou dar'st demand.
ASIA   Who made the living world?
DEMOGORGON   God.
ASIA   Who made all
   That it contains? thought, passion, reason, will,
   Imagination?
DEMOGORGON God: Almighty God.
ASIA Who made that sense which, when the winds of Spring
   In rarest visitation, or the voice
   Of one belovèd heard in youth alone,
   Fills the faint eyes with falling tears which dim
   The radiant looks of unbewailing flowers,
   And leaves this peopled earth a solitude
   When it returns no more?
DEMOGORGON   Merciful God.
ASIA   And who made terror, madness, crime, remorse,
   Which from the links of the great chain of things,
   To every thought within the mind of man
   Sway and drag heavily, and each one reels
   Under the load towards the pit of death;
   Abandoned hope, and love that turns to hate;
   And self-contempt, bitterer to drink than blood;
   Pain, whose unheeded and familiar speech
   Is howling, and keen shrieks, day after day;
   And Hell, or the sharp fear of Hell?

DEMOGORGON He reigns.

ASIA Utter his name: a world pining in pain
  Asks but his name: curses shall drag him down.

DEMOGORGON He reigns.

ASIA I feel, I know it: who?

DEMOGORGON He reigns.

ASIA Who reigns? There was the Heaven and Earth at first,
  And Light and Love; then Saturn, from whose throne
  Time fell, an envious shadow: such the state
  Of the earth's primal spirits beneath his sway,
  As the calm joy of flowers and living leaves
  Before the wind or sun has withered them
  And semivital worms; but he refused
  The birthright of their being, knowledge, power,
  The skill which wields the elements, the thought
  Which pierces this dim universe like light,
  Self-empire, and the majesty of love;
  For thirst of which they fainted. Then Prometheus
  Gave wisdom, which is strength, to Jupiter,
  And with this law alone, 'Let man be free,'
  Clothed him with the dominion of wide Heaven.
  To know nor faith, nor love, nor law; to be
  Omnipotent but friendless is to reign;
  And Jove now reigned; for on the race of man
  First famine, and then toil, and then disease,
  Strife, wounds, and ghastly death unseen before,
  Fell; and the unseasonable seasons drove
  With alternating shafts of frost and fire,
  Their shelterless, pale tribes to mountain caves:
  And in their desert hearts fierce wants he sent,
  And mad disquietudes, and shadows idle
  Of unreal good, which levied mutual war,
  So ruining the lair wherein they raged.
  Prometheus saw, and waked the legioned hopes
  Which sleep within folded Elysian flowers,
  Nepenthe, Moly, Amaranth, fadeless blooms,

That they might hide with thin and rainbow wings
The shape of Death; and Love he sent to bind
The disunited tendrils of that vine
Which bears the wine of life, the human heart;
And he tamed fire which, like some beast of prey,
Most terrible, but lovely, played beneath
The frown of man; and tortured to his will
Iron and gold, the slaves and signs of power,
And gems and poisons, and all subtlest forms
Hidden beneath the mountains and the waves.
He gave man speech, and speech created thought,
Which is the measure of the universe;
And Science struck the thrones of earth and heaven,
Which shook, but fell not; and the harmonious mind
Poured itself forth in all-prophetic song;
And music lifted up the listening spirit
Until it walked, exempt from mortal care,
Godlike, o'er the clear billows of sweet sound;
And human hands first mimicked and then mocked,
With moulded limbs more lovely than its own,
The human form, till marble grew divine;
And mothers, gazing, drank the love men see
Reflected in their race, behold, and perish.
He told the hidden power of herbs and springs,
And Disease drank and slept. Death grew like sleep.
He taught the implicated orbits woven
Of the wide-wandering stars; and how the sun
Changes his lair, and by what secret spell
The pale moon is transformed, when her broad eye
Gazes not on the interlunar sea:
He taught to rule, as life directs the limbs,
The tempest-wingèd chariots of the Ocean,
And the Celt knew the Indian. Cities then
Were built, and through their snow-like columns flowed
The warm winds, and the azure aether shone,
And the blue sea and shadowy hills were seen.

Such, the alleviations of his state,
Prometheus gave to man, for which he hangs
Withering in destined pain: but who rains down
Evil, the immedicable plague, which, while
Man looks on his creation like a God
And sees that it is glorious, drives him on,
The wreck of his own will, the scorn of earth,
The outcast, the abandoned, the alone?
Not Jove: while yet his frown shook Heaven, ay, when
His adversary from adamantine chains
Cursed him, he trembled like a slave. Declare
Who is his master? Is he too a slave?

DEMOGORGON   All spirits are enslaved which serve things evil:
Thou knowest if Jupiter be such or no.

ASIA   Whom calledst thou God?

DEMOGORGON   I spoke but as ye speak,
For Jove is the supreme of living things.

ASIA   Who is the master of the slave?

DEMOGORGON   If the abysm
Could vomit forth its secrets . . . But a voice
Is wanting, the deep truth is imageless;
For what would it avail to bid thee gaze
On the revolving world? What to bid speak
Fate, Time, Occasion, Chance, and Change? To these
All things are subject but eternal Love.

ASIA   So much I asked before, and my heart gave
The response thou hast given; and of such truths
Each to itself must be the oracle.
One more demand; and do thou answer me
As mine own soul would answer, did it know
That which I ask. Prometheus shall arise
Henceforth the sun of this rejoicing world:
When shall the destined hour arrive?

DEMOGORGON   Behold!

SPIRIT OF THE HOUR   Soon as the sound had ceased whose
                               thunder filled
The abysses of the sky and the wide earth,
There was a change: the impalpable thin air
And the all-circling sunlight were transformed,
As if the sense of love dissolved in them
Had folded itself round the spherèd world.
My vision then grew clear, and I could see
Into the mysteries of the universe:
Dizzy as with delight I floated down,
Winnowing the lightsome air with languid plumes,
My coursers sought their birthplace in the sun,
Where they henceforth will live exempt from toil,
Pasturing flowers of vegetable fire;
And where my moonlike car will stand within
A temple, gazed upon by Phidian forms
Of thee, and Asia, and the Earth, and me,
And you fair nymphs looking the love we feel,—
In memory of the tidings it has borne,—
Beneath a dome fretted with graven flowers,
Poised on twelve columns of resplendent stone,
And open to the bright and liquid sky.
Yoked to it by an amphisbaenic snake
The likeness of those wingèd steeds will mock
The flight from which they find repose. Alas,
Whither has wandered now my partial tongue
When all remains untold which ye would hear?
As I have said, I floated to the earth:
It was, as it is still, the pain of bliss
To move, to breathe, to be; I wandering went
Among the haunts and dwellings of mankind,
And first was disappointed not to see
Such mighty change as I had felt within

Expressed in outward things; but soon I looked,
And behold, thrones were kingless, and men walked
One with the other even as spirits do,
None fawned, none trampled; hate, disdain, or fear,
Self-love or self-contempt, on human brows
No more inscribed, as o'er the gate of hell,
'All hope abandon ye who enter here';
None frowned, none trembled, none with eager fear
Gazed on another's eye of cold command,
Until the subject of a tyrant's will
Became, worse fate, the abject of his own,
Which spurred him, like an outspent horse, to death.
[. . .]
The loathsome mask has fallen, the man remains
Sceptreless, free, uncircumscribed, but man
Equal, unclassed, tribeless, and nationless,
Exempt from awe, worship, degree, the king
Over himself; just, gentle, wise: but man
Passionless?—no, yet free from guilt or pain,
Which were, for his will made or suffered them,
Nor yet exempt, though ruling them like slaves,
From chance, and death, and mutability,
The clogs of that which else might oversoar
The loftiest star of unascended heaven,
Pinnacled dim in the intense inane.

THE EARTH   The joy, the triumph, the delight, the madness!
    The boundless, overflowing, bursting gladness,
  The vaporous exultation not to be confined!
    Ha! ha! the animation of delight
    Which wraps me, like an atmosphere of light,
  And bears me as a cloud is borne by its own wind.
THE MOON   Brother mine, calm wanderer,
    Happy globe of land and air,
  Some Spirit is darted like a beam from thee,
    Which penetrates my frozen frame,
    And passes with the warmth of flame,
  With love, and odour, and deep melody
    Through me, through me!
THE EARTH   Ha! ha! the caverns of my hollow mountains,
    My cloven fire-crags, sound-exulting fountains
  Laugh with a vast and inextinguishable laughter.
    The oceans, and the deserts, and the abysses,
    And the deep air's unmeasured wildernesses,
  Answer from all their clouds and billows, echoing after.

    They cry aloud as I do. Sceptred curse,
    Who all our green and azure universe
  Threatenedst to muffle round with black destruction, sending
    A solid cloud to rain hot thunderstones,
    And splinter and knead down my children's bones
  All I bring forth, to one void mass battering and blending,—

    Until each crag-like tower, and storied column,
    Palace, and obelisk, and temple solemn,
  My imperial mountains crowned with cloud, and snow, and fire;
    My sea-like forests, every blade and blossom
    Which finds a grave or cradle in my bosom,
  Were stamped by thy strong hate into a lifeless mire:

How art thou sunk, withdrawn, covered, drunk up
　　By thirsty nothing, as the brackish cup
Drained by a desert-troop, a little drop for all;
　　And from beneath, around, within, above,
　　Filling thy void annihilation, love
Burst in like light on caves cloven by the thunder-ball.
THE MOON　　The snow upon my lifeless mountains
　　Is loosened into living fountains,
My solid oceans flow, and sing, and shine:
　　A spirit from my heart bursts forth,
　　It clothes with unexpected birth
My cold bare bosom: Oh! it must be thine
　　On mine, on mine!

　　Gazing on thee I feel, I know
　　Green stalks burst forth, and bright flowers grow,
And living shapes upon my bosom move:
　　Music is in the sea and air,
　　Wingèd clouds soar here and there,
Dark with the rain new buds are dreaming of:
　　'Tis love, all love!

THE EARTH　It interpenetrates my granite mass,
　　Through tangled roots and trodden clay doth pass
Into the utmost leaves and delicatest flowers;
　　Upon the winds, among the clouds 'tis spread,
　　It wakes a life in the forgotten dead,
They breathe a spirit up from their obscurest bowers.

　　And like a storm bursting its cloudy prison
　　With thunder, and with whirlwind, has arisen
Out of the lampless caves of unimagined being:
　　With earthquake shock and swiftness making shiver
　　Thought's stagnant chaos, unremoved for ever,
Till hate, and fear, and pain, light-vanquished shadows, fleeing,

　　Leave Man, who was a many-sided mirror,
　　Which could distort to many a shape of error,

This true fair world of things, a sea reflecting love;
　Which over all his kind, as the sun's heaven
　Gliding o'er ocean, smooth, serene, and even,
Darting from starry depths radiance and life, doth move:

　Leave Man, even as a leprous child is left,
　Who follows a sick beast to some warm cleft
Of rocks, through which the might of healing springs is poured;
　Then when it wanders home with rosy smile,
　Unconscious, and its mother fears awhile
It is a spirit, then, weeps on her child restored.

　Man, oh, not men! a chain of linkèd thought,
　Of love and might to be divided not,
Compelling the elements with adamantine stress;
　As the sun rules, even with a tyrant's gaze,
　The unquiet republic of the maze
Of planets, struggling fierce towards heaven's free wilderness.

　Man, one harmonious soul of many a soul,
　Whose nature is its own divine control,
Where all things flow to all, as rivers to the sea;
　Familiar acts are beautiful through love;
　Labour, and pain, and grief, in life's green grove
Sport like tame beasts, none knew how gentle they could be!

　His will, with all mean passions, bad delights,
　And selfish cares, its trembling satellites,
A spirit ill to guide, but mighty to obey,
　Is as a tempest-wingèd ship, whose helm
　Love rules, through waves which dare not overwhelm,
Forcing life's wildest shores to own its sovereign sway.

　All things confess his strength. Through the cold mass
　Of marble and of colour his dreams pass;
Bright threads whence mothers weave the robes their children wear;
　Language is a perpetual Orphic song,
　Which rules with Dædal harmony a throng
Of thoughts and forms, which else senseless and shapeless were.

The lightning is his slave; heaven's utmost deep
Gives up her stars, and like a flock of sheep
They pass before his eye, are numbered, and roll on!
The tempest is his steed, he strides the air;
And the abyss shouts from her depth laid bare,
Heaven, hast thou secrets? Man unveils me; I have none.

[...]

DEMOGORGON   Thou, Earth, calm empire of a happy soul,
Sphere of divinest shapes and harmonies,
Beautiful orb! gathering as thou dost roll
The love which paves thy path along the skies:
THE EARTH   I hear: I am as a drop of dew that dies.
DEMOGORGON   Thou, Moon, which gazest on the nightly Earth
With wonder, as it gazes upon thee;
Whilst each to men, and beasts, and the swift birth
Of birds, is beauty, love, calm, harmony:
THE MOON   I hear: I am a leaf shaken by thee!
DEMOGORGON   Ye Kings of suns and stars, Dæmons and Gods,
Aetherial Dominations, who possess
Elysian, windless, fortunate abodes
Beyond Heaven's constellated wilderness:
A VOICE FROM ABOVE   Our great Republic hears, we are blest,
and bless.
DEMOGORGON   Ye happy Dead, whom beams of brightest verse
Are clouds to hide, not colours to portray,
Whether your nature is that universe
Which once ye saw and suffered—
A VOICE FROM BENEATH   Or as they
Whom we have left, we change and pass away.
DEMOGORGON   Ye elemental Genii, who have homes
From man's high mind even to the central stone
Of sullen lead; from heaven's star-fretted domes
To the dull weed some sea-worm battens on:
A CONFUSED VOICE   We hear: thy words waken Oblivion.
DEMOGORGON   Spirits, whose homes are flesh: ye beasts and
birds,

Ye worms, and fish; ye living leaves and buds;
  Lightning and wind; and ye untameable herds,
    Meteors and mists, which throng air's solitudes:—
A VOICE   Thy voice to us is wind among still woods.
DEMOGORGON   Man, who wert once a despot and a slave;
    A dupe and a deceiver; a decay;
  A traveller from the cradle to the grave
    Through the dim night of this immortal day:
ALL   Speak: thy strong words may never pass away.
DEMOGORGON   This is the day, which down the void abysm
  At the Earth-born's spell yawns for Heaven's despotism,
    And Conquest is dragged captive through the deep:
  Love, from its awful throne of patient power
  In the wise heart, from the last giddy hour
    Of dread endurance, from the slippery, steep,
  And narrow verge of crag-like agony, springs
  And folds over the world its healing wings.

Gentleness, Virtue, Wisdom, and Endurance,
These are the seals of that most firm assurance
    Which bars the pit over Destruction's strength;
And if, with infirm hand, Eternity,
Mother of many acts and hours, should free
    The serpent that would clasp her with his length;
These are the spells by which to reassume
An empire o'er the disentangled doom.

To suffer woes which Hope thinks infinite;
To forgive wrongs darker than death or night;
    To defy Power, which seems omnipotent;
To love, and bear; to hope till Hope creates
From its own wreck the thing it contemplates;
    Neither to change, nor falter, nor repent;
This, like thy glory, Titan, is to be
Good, great and joyous, beautiful and free;
This is alone Life, Joy, Empire, and Victory.

An Exhortation

Chameleons feed on light and air:
   Poets' food is love and fame:
If in this wide world of care
   Poets could but find the same
With as little toil as they,
   Would they ever change their hue
   As the light chameleons do,
Suiting it to every ray
   Twenty times a day?

Poets are on this cold earth,
   As chameleons might be,
Hidden from their early birth
   In a cave beneath the sea;
Where light is, chameleons change:
   Where love is not, poets do:
   Fame is love disguised: if few
Find either, never think it strange
   That poets range.

Yet dare not stain with wealth or power
   A poet's free and heavenly mind:
If bright chameleons should devour
   Any food but beams and wind,
They would grow as earthly soon
   As their brother lizards are.
   Children of a sunnier star,
Spirits from beyond the moon,
   O, refuse the boon!

To a Skylark

Hail to thee, blithe Spirit!
   Bird thou never wert,
That from Heaven, or near it,
   Pourest thy full heart
In profuse strains of unpremeditated art.

Higher still and higher
   From the earth thou springest
Like a cloud of fire;
   The blue deep thou wingest,
And singing still dost soar, and soaring ever singest.

In the golden lightning
   Of the sunken sun
O'er which clouds are bright'ning,
   Thou dost float and run,
Like an unbodied joy whose race is just begun.

The pale purple even
   Melts around thy flight;
Like a star of Heaven
   In the broad daylight
Thou art unseen, but yet I hear thy shrill delight,

Keen as are the arrows
   Of that silver sphere,
Whose intense lamp narrows
   In the white dawn clear
Until we hardly see—we feel that it is there.

All the earth and air
   With thy voice is loud,
As, when night is bare,
   From one lonely cloud
The moon rains out her beams, and Heaven is overflowed.

What thou art we know not;
    What is most like thee?
From rainbow clouds there flow not
    Drops so bright to see
As from thy presence showers a rain of melody.

Like a Poet hidden
    In the light of thought,
Singing hymns unbidden,
    Till the world is wrought
To sympathy with hopes and fears it heeded not:

Like a high-born maiden
    In a palace tower,
Soothing her love-laden
    Soul in secret hour
With music sweet as love, which overflows her bower:

Like a glow-worm golden
    In a dell of dew,
Scattering unbeholden
    Its aerial hue
Among the flowers and grass, which screen it from the view!

Like a rose embowered
    In its own green leaves,
By warm winds deflowered,
    Till the scent it gives
Makes faint with too much sweet these heavy-wingèd thieves.

Sound of vernal showers
    On the twinkling grass,
Rain-awakened flowers,
    All that ever was
Joyous, and clear, and fresh, thy music doth surpass:

Teach us, Sprite or Bird,
    What sweet thoughts are thine:
I have never heard
    Praise of love or wine
That panted forth a flood of rapture so divine.

Chorus Hymeneal,
    Or triumphal chant,
Matched with thine would be all
    But an empty vaunt,
A thing wherein we feel there is some hidden want.

What objects are the fountains
    Of thy happy strain?
What fields, or waves, or mountains?
    What shapes of sky or plain?
What love of thine own kind? what ignorance of pain?

With thy clear keen joyance
    Languor cannot be:
Shadow of annoyance
    Never came near thee:
Thou lovest—but ne'er knew love's sad satiety.

Waking or asleep,
    Thou of death must deem
Things more true and deep
    Than we mortals dream,
Or how could thy notes flow in such a crystal stream?

We look before and after,
    And pine for what is not:
Our sincerest laughter
    With some pain is fraught;
Our sweetest songs are those that tell of saddest thought.

Yet if we could scorn
   Hate, and pride, and fear;
If we were things born
   Not to shed a tear,
I know not how thy joy we ever should come near.

Better than all measures
   Of delightful sound,
Better than all treasures
   That in books are found,
Thy skill to poet were, thou scorner of the ground!

Teach me half the gladness
   That thy brain must know,
Such harmonious madness
   From my lips would flow
The world should listen then—as I am listening now.

Letter to Maria Gisborne
Leghorn, July 1, 1820

The spider spreads her webs, whether she be
In poet's tower, cellar, or barn, or tree;
The silk-worm in the dark green mulberry leaves
His winding sheet and cradle ever weaves;
So I, a thing whom moralists call worm,
Sit spinning still round this decaying form,
From the fine threads of rare and subtle thought—
No net of words in garish colours wrought
To catch the idle buzzers of the day—
But a soft cell, where when that fades away,
Memory may clothe in wings my living name
And feed it with the asphodels of fame,
Which in those hearts which must remember me
Grow, making love an immortality.

    Whoever should behold me now, I wist,
Would think I were a mighty mechanist,
Bent with sublime Archimedean art
To breathe a soul into the iron heart
Of some machine portentous, or strange gin,
Which by the force of figured spells might win
Its way over the sea, and sport therein;
For round the walls are hung dread engines, such
As Vulcan never wrought for Jove to clutch
Ixion or the Titan:—or the quick
Wit of that man of God, St. Dominic,
To convince Atheist—Turk, or Heretic,
Or those in philanthropic council met,
Who thought to pay some interest for the debt
They owed to Jesus Christ for their salvation,
By giving a faint foretaste of damnation
To Shakespeare, Sidney, Spenser, and the rest

Who made our land an island of the blest,
When lamp-like Spain, who now relumes her fire
On Freedom's hearth, grew dim with Empire:—
With thumbscrews, wheels, with tooth and spike and jag,
Which fishers found under the utmost crag
Of Cornwall and the storm-encompassed isles,
Where to the sky the rude sea rarely smiles
Unless in treacherous wrath, as on the morn
When the exulting elements in scorn,
Satiated with destroyed destruction, lay
Sleeping in beauty on their mangled prey,
As panthers sleep;—and other strange and dread
Magical forms the brick floor overspread,—
Proteus transformed to metal did not make
More figures, or more strange; nor did he take
Such shapes of unintelligible brass,
Or heap himself in such a horrid mass
Of tin and iron not to be understood,
And forms of unimaginable wood,
To puzzle Tubal Cain and all his brood:
Great screws, and cones, and wheels, and groovèd blocks,
The elements of what will stand the shocks
Of wave and wind and time.—Upon the table
More knacks and quips there be than I am able
To catalogize in this verse of mine:—
A pretty bowl of wood—not full of wine,
But quicksilver; that dew which the gnomes drink
When at their subterranean toil they swink,
Pledging the demons of the earthquake, who
Reply to them in lava—cry halloo!
And call out to the cities o'er their head,—
Roofs, towers, and shrines, the dying and the dead,
Crash through the chinks of earth—and then all quaff
Another rouse, and hold their sides and laugh.
This quicksilver no gnome has drunk—within
The walnut bowl it lies, veinèd and thin,

In colour like the wake of light that stains
The Tuscan deep, when from the moist moon rains
The inmost shower of its white fire—the breeze
Is still—blue Heaven smiles over the pale seas.
And in this bowl of quicksilver—for I
Yield to the impulse of an infancy
Outlasting manhood—I have made to float
A rude idealism of a paper boat—
A hollow screw with cogs—Henry will know
The thing I mean and laugh at me,—if so
He fears not I should do more mischief.—Next
Lie bills and calculations much perplexed,
With steam-boats, frigates, and machinery quaint
Traced over them in blue and yellow paint.
Then comes a range of mathematical
Instruments, for plans nautical and statical;
A heap of rosin, a queer broken glass
With ink in it;—a china cup that was
What it will never be again, I think,
A thing from which sweet lips were wont to drink
The liquor doctors rail at—and which I
Will quaff in spite of them—and when we die
We'll toss up who died first of drinking tea,
And cry out,—'Heads or tails?' where'er we be.
Near that a dusty paint-box, some odd hooks,
A half-burnt match, an ivory block, three books,
Where conic sections, spherics, logarithms,
To great Laplace, from Saunderson and Sims,
Lie heaped in their harmonious disarray
Of figures,—disentangle them who may.
Baron de Tott's Memoirs beside them lie,
And some odd volumes of old chemistry.
Near those a most inexplicable thing,
With lead in the middle—I'm conjecturing
How to make Henry understand; but no—
I'll leave, as Spenser says, with many mo,

This secret in the pregnant womb of time,
Too vast a matter for so weak a rhyme.

And here like some weird Archimage sit I,
Plotting dark spells, and devilish enginery,
The self-impelling steam-wheels of the mind
Which pump up oaths from clergymen, and grind
The gentle spirit of our meek reviews
Into a powdery foam of salt abuse,
Ruffling the ocean of their self-content;—
I sit—and smile or sigh as is my bent,
But not for them—Libeccio rushes round
With an inconstant and an idle sound,
I heed him more than them—the thunder-smoke
Is gathering on the mountains, like a cloak
Folded athwart their shoulders broad and bare;
The ripe corn under the undulating air
Undulates like an ocean;—and the vines
Are trembling wide in all their trellised lines—
The murmur of the awakening sea doth fill
The empty pauses of the blast;—the hill
Looks hoary through the white electric rain,
And from the glens beyond, in sullen strain,
The interrupted thunder howls; above
One chasm of Heaven smiles, like the eye of Love
On the unquiet world;—while such things are,
How could one worth your friendship heed the war
Of worms? the shriek of the world's carrion jays,
Their censure, or their wonder, or their praise?

You are not here! the quaint witch Memory sees,
In vacant chairs, your absent images,
And points where once you sat, and now should be
But are not.—I demand if ever we
Shall meet as then we met;—and she replies,
Veiling in awe her second-sighted eyes;
'I know the past alone—but summon home

My sister Hope,—she speaks of all to come.'
But I, an old diviner, who knew well
Every false verse of that sweet oracle,
Turned to the sad enchantress once again,
And sought a respite from my gentle pain,
In citing every passage o'er and o'er
Of our communion—how on the sea-shore
We watched the ocean and the sky together,
Under the roof of blue Italian weather;
How I ran home through last year's thunder-storm,
And felt the transverse lightning linger warm
Upon my cheek—and how we often made
Feasts for each other, where good will outweighed
The frugal luxury of our country cheer,
As well it might, were it less firm and clear
Than ours must ever be;—and how we spun
A shroud of talk to hide us from the sun
Of this familiar life, which seems to be
But is not:—or is but quaint mockery
Of all we would believe; and sadly blame
The jarring and inexplicable frame
Of this wrong world:—and then anatomize
The purposes and thoughts of men whose eyes
Were closed in distant years;—or widely guess
The issue of the earth's great business,
When we shall be as we no longer are;
Like babbling gossips safe, who hear the war
Of winds, and sigh, but tremble not;—or how
You listened to some interrupted flow
Of visionary rhyme,—in joy and pain
Struck from the inmost fountains of my brain,
With little skill perhaps;—or how we sought
Those deepest wells of passion or of thought
Wrought by wise poets in the waste of years,
Staining their sacred waters with our tears;
Quenching a thirst ever to be renewed!

Or how I, wisest lady! then endued
The language of a land which now is free,
And, winged with thoughts of truth and majesty,
Flits round the tyrant's sceptre like a cloud,
And bursts the peopled prisons, and cries aloud,
'My name is Legion!'—that majestic tongue
Which Calderon over the desert flung
Of ages and of nations; and which found
An echo in our hearts, and with the sound
Startled oblivion;—thou wert then to me
As is a nurse—when inarticulately
A child would talk as its grown parents do.
If living winds the rapid clouds pursue,
If hawks chase doves through the aethereal way,
Huntsmen the innocent deer, and beasts their prey,
Why should not we rouse with the spirit's blast
Out of the forest of the pathless past
These recollected pleasures?

                                    You are now
In London, that great sea, whose ebb and flow
At once is deaf and loud, and on the shore
Vomits its wrecks, and still howls on for more.
Yet in its depth what treasures! You will see
That which was Godwin,—greater none than he
Though fallen—and fallen on evil times—to stand
Among the spirits of our age and land,
Before the dread tribunal of *to come*
The foremost,—while Rebuke cowers pale and dumb.
You will see Coleridge—he who sits obscure
In the exceeding lustre and the pure
Intense irradiation of a mind,
Which, with its own internal lightning blind,
Flags wearily through darkness and despair—
A cloud-encircled meteor of the air,
A hooded eagle among blinking owls.—

You will see Hunt—one of those happy souls
Which are the salt of the earth, and without whom
This world would smell like what it is—a tomb;
Who is, what others seem; his room no doubt
Is still adorned with many a cast from Shout,
With graceful flowers tastefully placed about;
And coronals of bay from ribbons hung,
And brighter wreaths in neat disorder flung;
The gifts of the most learned among some dozens
Of female friends, sisters-in-law, and cousins.
And there is he with his eternal puns,
Which beat the dullest brain for smiles, like duns
Thundering for money at a poet's door;
Alas! it is no use to say, 'I'm poor!'
Or oft in graver mood, when he will look
Things wiser than were ever read in book,
Except in Shakespeare's wisest tenderness.—
You will see Hogg,—and I cannot express
His virtues,—though I know that they are great,
Because he locks, then barricades the gate
Within which they inhabit;—of his wit
And wisdom, you'll cry out when you are bit.
He is a pearl within an oyster shell,
One of the richest of the deep;—and there
Is English Peacock, with his mountain fair,
Turned into a Flamingo;—that shy bird
That gleams i' the Indian air—have you not heard
When a man marries, dies, or turns Hindoo,
His best friends hear no more of him?—but you
Will see him, and will like him too, I hope,
With the milk-white Snowdonian Antelope
Matched with this cameleopard; his fine wit
Makes such a wound, the knife is lost in it;
A strain too learnèd for a shallow age,
Too wise for selfish bigots; let his page,
Which charms the chosen spirits of the time,

Fold itself up for the serener clime
Of years to come, and find its recompense
In that just expectation.—Wit and sense,
Virtue and human knowledge; all that might
Make this dull world a business of delight,
Are all combined in Horace Smith.—And these,
With some exceptions, which I need not tease
Your patience by descanting on,—are all
You and I know in London.

                    I recall
My thoughts, and bid you look upon the night.
As water does a sponge, so the moonlight
Fills the void, hollow, universal air—
What see you?—unpavilioned Heaven is fair,
Whether the moon, into her chamber gone,
Leaves midnight to the golden stars, or wan
Climbs with diminished beams the azure steep;
Or whether clouds sail o'er the inverse deep,
Piloted by the many-wandering blast,
And the rare stars rush through them dim and fast:—
All this is beautiful in every land.—
But what see you beside?—a shabby stand
Of Hackney coaches—a brick house or wall
Fencing some lonely court, white with the scrawl
Of our unhappy politics;—or worse—
A wretched woman reeling by, whose curse
Mixed with the watchman's, partner of her trade,
You must accept in place of serenade—
Or yellow-haired Pollonia murmuring
To Henry, some unutterable thing.
I see a chaos of green leaves and fruit
Built round dark caverns, even to the root
Of the living stems that feed them—in whose bowers
There sleep in their dark dew the folded flowers;
Beyond, the surface of the unsickled corn

Trembles not in the slumbering air, and borne
In circles quaint, and ever-changing dance,
Like wingèd stars the fire-flies flash and glance,
Pale in the open moonshine, but each one
Under the dark trees seems a little sun,
A meteor tamed; a fixed star gone astray
From the silver regions of the milky way;—
Afar the Contadino's song is heard,
Rude, but made sweet by distance—and a bird
Which cannot be the Nightingale, and yet
I know none else that sings so sweet as it
At this late hour;—and then all is still—
Now Italy or London, which you will!

Next winter you must pass with me; I'll have
My house by that time turned into a grave
Of dead despondence and low-thoughted care,
And all the dreams which our tormentors are;
Oh! that Hunt, Hogg, Peacock, and Smith were there,
With everything belonging to them fair!—
We will have books, Spanish, Italian, Greek;
And ask one week to make another week
As like his father, as I'm unlike mine,
Which is not his fault, as you may divine.
Though we eat little flesh and drink no wine,
Yet let's be merry: we'll have tea and toast;
Custards for supper, and an endless host
Of syllabubs and jellies and mince-pies,
And other such lady-like luxuries,—
Feasting on which we will philosophize!
And we'll have fires out of the Grand Duke's wood,
To thaw the six weeks' winter in our blood.
And then we'll talk;—what shall we talk about?
Oh! there are themes enough for many a bout
Of thought-entangled descant;—as to nerves—
With cones and parallelograms and curves

I've sworn to strangle them if once they dare
To bother me—when you are with me there.
And they shall never more sip laudanum,
From Helicon or Himeros;—well, come,
And in despite of God and of the devil,
We'll make our friendly philosophic revel
Outlast the leafless time; till buds and flowers
Warn the obscure inevitable hours,
Sweet meeting by sad parting to renew;—
'To-morrow to fresh woods and pastures new.'

Sonnet: To the Republic of Benevento

Nor happiness, nor majesty, nor fame,
Nor peace, nor strength, nor skill in arms or arts,
Shepherd those herds whom tyranny makes tame;
Verse echoes not one beating of their hearts,
History is but the shadow of their shame,
Art veils her glass, or from the pageant starts
As to oblivion their blind millions fleet,
Staining that Heaven with obscene imagery
Of their own likeness. What are numbers knit
By force or custom? Man who man would be,
Must rule the empire of himself; in it
Must be supreme, establishing his throne
On vanquished will, quelling the anarchy
Of hopes and fears, being himself alone.

The Flower that Smiles Today

The flower that smiles today
    To-morrow dies;
All that we wish to stay
    Tempts and then flies.
What is this world's delight?
Lightning that mocks the night,
   Brief even as bright.

Virtue, how frail it is!
    Friendship how rare!
Love, how it sells poor bliss
    For proud despair!
But we, though soon they fall,
Survive their joy, and all
   Which ours we call.

Whilst skies are blue and bright,
    Whilst flowers are gay,
Whilst eyes that change ere night
    Make glad the day;
Whilst yet the calm hours creep,
Dream thou—and from thy sleep
   Then wake to weep.

from Epipsychidion

[lines 130–89]

Spouse! Sister! Angel! Pilot of the Fate
Whose course has been so starless! O too late
Belovèd! O too soon adored, by me!
For in the fields of immortality
My spirit should at first have worshipped thine,
A divine presence in a place divine;
Or should have moved beside it on this earth,
A shadow of that substance, from its birth;
But not as now:—I love thee; yes, I feel
That on the fountain of my heart a seal
Is set, to keep its waters pure and bright
For thee, since in those *tears* thou hast delight.
We—are we not formed, as notes of music are,
For one another, though dissimilar;
such difference without discord, as can make
Those sweetest sounds, in which all spirits shake
As trembling leaves in a continuous air?

Thy wisdom speaks in me, and bids me dare
Beacon the rocks on which high hearts are wrecked.
I never was attached to that great sect,
Whose doctrine is, that each one should select
Out of the crowd a mistress or a friend,
And all the rest, though fair and wise, commend
To cold oblivion, though it is in the code
Of modern morals, and the beaten road
Which those poor slaves with weary footsteps tread,
Who travel to their home among the dead
By the broad highway of the world, and so
With one chained friend, perhaps a jealous foe,
The dreariest and the longest journey go.

True Love in this differs from gold and clay,
That to divide is not to take away.
Love is like understanding, that grows bright,
Gazing on many truths; 'tis like thy light,
Imagination! which from earth and sky,
And from the depths of human fantasy,
As from a thousand prisms and mirrors, fills
The Universe with glorious beams, and kills
Error, the worm, with many a sun-like arrow
Of its reverberated lightning. Narrow
The heart that loves, the brain that contemplates,
The life that wears, the spirit that creates
One object, and one form, and builds thereby
A sepulchre for its eternity.

Mind from its object differs most in this:
Evil from good; misery from happiness;
The baser from the nobler; the impure
And frail, from what is clear and must endure.
If you divide suffering and dross, you may
Diminish till it is consumed away;
If you divide pleasure and love and thought,
Each part exceeds the whole; and we know not
How much, while any yet remains unshared,
Of pleasure may be gained, of sorrow spared:
This truth is that deep well, whence sages draw
The unenvied light of hope; the eternal law
By which those live, to whom this world of life
Is as a garden ravaged, and whose strife
Tills for the promise of a later birth
The wilderness of this Elysian earth.

To —

Music, when soft voices die,
Vibrates in the memory—
Odours, when sweet violets sicken,
Live within the sense they quicken.

Rose leaves, when the rose is dead,
Are heaped for the belovèd's bed;
And so thy thoughts, when thou art gone,
Love itself shall slumber on.

Song

Rarely, rarely, comest thou,
    Spirit of Delight!
Wherefore hast thou left me now
    Many a day and night?
Many a weary night and day
'Tis since thou are fled away.

How shall ever one like me
    Win thee back again?
With the joyous and the free
    Thou wilt scoff at pain.
Spirit false! thou hast forgot
All but those who need thee not.

As a lizard with the shade
    Of a trembling leaf,
Thou with sorrow art dismayed;
    Even the sighs of grief
Reproach thee, that thou art not near,
And reproach thou wilt not hear.

Let me set my mournful ditty
    To a merry measure;
Thou wilt never come for pity,
    Thou wilt come for pleasure;
Pity then will cut away
Those cruel wings, and thou wilt stay.

I love all that thou lovest,
    Spirit of Delight!
The fresh Earth in new leaves dressed,
    And the starry night;
Autumn evening, and the morn
When the golden mists are born.

I love snow, and all the forms
    Of the radiant frost;
I love waves, and winds, and storms,
    Everything almost
Which is Nature's, and may be
Untainted by man's misery.

I love tranquil solitude,
    And such society
As is quiet, wise, and good;
    Between thee and me
What difference? but thou dost possess
The things I seek, not love them less.

I love Love—though he has wings,
    And like light can flee,
But above all other things,
    Spirit, I love thee—
Thou art Love and Life! Oh, come,
Make once more my heart thy home.

One Word is Too Oft Profaned

One word is too often profaned
　　For me to profane it,
One feeling too falsely disdained
　　For thee to disdain it;
One hope is too like despair
　　For prudence to smother,
And pity from thee more dear
　　Than that from another.

I can give not what men call love,
　　But wilt thou accept not
The worship the heart lifts above
　　And the Heavens reject not,—
The desire of the moth for the star,
　　Of the night for the morrow,
The devotion to something afar
　　From the sphere of our sorrow?

Adonais

I

I weep for Adonais—he is dead!
O, weep for Adonais! though our tears
Thaw not the frost which binds so dear a head!
And thou, sad Hour, selected from all years
To mourn our loss, rouse thy obscure compeers,
And teach them thine own sorrow, say: 'With me
Died Adonais; till the Future dares
Forget the Past, his fate and fame shall be
An echo and a light unto eternity!'

II

Where wert thou, mighty Mother, when he lay,
When thy Son lay, pierced by the shaft which flies
In darkness? where was lorn Urania
When Adonais died? With veilèd eyes,
'Mid listening Echoes, in her Paradise
She sate, while one, with soft enamoured breath,
Rekindled all the fading melodies
With which, like flowers that mock the corse beneath,
He had adorned and hid the coming bulk of Death.

III

O, weep for Adonais—he is dead!
Wake, melancholy Mother, wake and weep!
Yet wherefore? Quench within their burning bed
Thy fiery tears, and let thy loud heart keep
Like his, a mute and uncomplaining sleep;
For he is gone, where all things wise and fair
Descend;—oh, dream not that the amorous Deep
Will yet restore him to the vital air;
Death feeds on his mute voice, and laughs at our despair.

IV

Most musical of mourners, weep again!
Lament anew, Urania!—He died,
Who was the Sire of an immortal strain,
Blind, old, and lonely, when his country's pride,
The priest, the slave, and the liberticide,
Trampled and mocked with many a loathèd rite
Of lust and blood; he went, unterrified,
Into the gulf of death; but his clear Sprite
Yet reigns o'er earth; the third among the sons of light.

V

Most musical of mourners, weep anew!
Not all to that bright station dared to climb;
And happier they their happiness who knew,
Whose tapers yet burn through that night of time
In which suns perished; others more sublime,
Struck by the envious wrath of man or god,
Have sunk, extinct in their refulgent prime;
And some yet live, treading the thorny road
Which leads, through toil and hate, to Fame's serene abode.

VI

But now, thy youngest, dearest one, has perished—
The nursling of thy widowhood, who grew,
Like a pale flower by some sad maiden cherished,
And fed with true-love tears, instead of dew;
Most musical of mourners, weep anew!
Thy extreme hope, the loveliest and the last,
The bloom, whose petals nipped before they blew
Died on the promise of the fruit, is waste;
The broken lily lies—the storm is overpast.

VII

To that high Capital, where kingly Death
Keeps his pale court in beauty and decay,
He came; and bought, with price of purest breath,
A grave among the eternal.—Come away!
Haste, while the vault of blue Italian day
Is yet his fitting charnel-roof! while still
He lies, as if in dewy sleep he lay;
Awake him not! surely he takes his fill
Of deep and liquid rest, forgetful of all ill.

VIII

He will awake no more, oh, never more!—
Within the twilight chamber spreads apace
The shadow of white Death, and at the door
Invisible Corruption waits to trace
His extreme way to her dim dwelling-place;
The eternal Hunger sits, but pity and awe
Soothe her pale rage, nor dares she to deface
So fair a prey, till darkness, and the law
Of change, shall o'er his sleep the mortal curtain draw.

IX

O, weep for Adonais!—The quick Dreams,
The passion-wingèd Ministers of thought,
Who were his flocks, whom near the living streams
Of his young spirit he fed, and whom he taught
The love which was its music, wander not,—
Wander no more, from kindling brain to brain,
But droop there, whence they sprung; and mourn their lot
Round the cold heart, where, after their sweet pain,
They ne'er will gather strength, or find a home again.

X

And one with trembling hands clasps his cold head,
And fans him with her moonlight wings, and cries;
'Our love, our hope, our sorrow, is not dead;
See, on the silken fringe of his faint eyes,
Like dew upon a sleeping flower, there lies
A tear some Dream has loosened from his brain.'
Lost Angel of a ruined Paradise!
She knew not 'twas her own; as with no stain
She faded, like a cloud which had outwept its rain.

XI

One from a lucid urn of starry dew
Washed his light limbs as if embalming them;
Another clipped her profuse locks, and threw
The wreath upon him, like an anadem,
Which frozen tears instead of pearls begem;
Another in her wilful grief would break
Her bow and wingèd reeds, as if to stem
A greater loss with one which was more weak;
And dull the barbed fire against his frozen cheek.

XII

Another Splendour on his mouth alit,
That mouth, whence it was wont to draw the breath
Which gave it strength to pierce the guarded wit,
And pass into the panting heart beneath
With lightning and with music: the damp death
Quenched its caress upon his icy lips;
And, as a dying meteor stains a wreath
Of moonlight vapour, which the cold night clips,
It flushed through his pale limbs, and passed to its eclipse.

XIII

And others came . . . Desires and Adorations,
Wingèd Persuasions and veiled Destinies,
Splendours, and Glooms, and glimmering Incarnations
Of hopes and fears, and twilight Phantasies;
And Sorrow, with her family of Sighs,
And Pleasure, blind with tears, led by the gleam
Of her own dying smile instead of eyes,
Came in slow pomp;—the moving pomp might seem
Like pageantry of mist on an autumnal stream.

XIV

All he had loved, and moulded into thought,
From shape, and hue, and odour, and sweet sound,
Lamented Adonais. Morning sought
Her eastern watch-tower, and her hair unbound,
Wet with the tears which should adorn the ground,
Dimmed the aereal eyes that kindle day;
Afar the melancholy thunder moaned,
Pale Ocean in unquiet slumber lay,
And the wild Winds flew round, sobbing in their dismay.

XV

Lost Echo sits amid the voiceless mountains,
And feeds her grief with his remembered lay,
And will no more reply to winds or fountains,
Or amorous birds perched on the young green spray,
Or herdsman's horn, or bell at closing day;
Since she can mimic not his lips, more dear
Than those for whose disdain she pined away
Into a shadow of all sounds:—a drear
Murmur, between their songs, is all the woodmen hear.

XVI

Grief made the young Spring wild, and she threw down
Her kindling buds, as if she Autumn were,
Or they dead leaves; since her delight is flown
For whom should she have waked the sullen year?
To Phoebus was not Hyacinth so dear
Nor to himself Narcissus, as to both
Thou, Adonais: wan they stand and sere
Amid the faint companions of their youth,
With dew all turned to tears; odour, to sighing ruth.

XVII

Thy spirit's sister, the lorn nightingale
Mourns not her mate with such melodious pain;
Not so the eagle, who like thee could scale
Heaven, and could nourish in the sun's domain
Her mighty youth with morning, doth complain,
Soaring and screaming round her empty nest,
As Albion wails for thee: the curse of Cain
Light on his head who pierced thy innocent breast,
And scared the angel soul that was its earthly guest!

XVIII

Ah, woe is me! Winter is come and gone,
But grief returns with the revolving year;
The airs and streams renew their joyous tone;
The ants, the bees, the swallows reappear;
Fresh leaves and flowers deck the dead Season's bier;
The amorous birds now pair in every brake,
And build their mossy homes in field and brere;
And the green lizard, and the golden snake,
Like unimprisoned flames, out of their trance awake.

XIX

Through wood and stream and field and hill and Ocean
A quickening life from the Earth's heart has burst
As it has ever done, with change and motion,
From the great morning of the world when first
God dawned on Chaos; in its stream immersed
The lamps of Heaven flash with a softer light;
All baser things pant with life's sacred thirst;
Diffuse themselves; and spend in love's delight
The beauty and the joy of their renewèd might.

XX

The leprous corpse touched by this spirit tender
Exhales itself in flowers of gentle breath;
Like incarnations of the stars, when splendour
Is changed to fragrance, they illumine death
And mock the merry worm that wakes beneath;
Nought we know, dies. Shall that alone which knows
Be as a sword consumed before the sheath
By sightless lightning?—the intense atom glows
A moment, then is quenched in a most cold repose.

XXI

Alas! that all we loved of him should be,
But for our grief, as if it had not been,
And grief itself be mortal! Woe is me!
Whence are we, and why are we? of what scene
The actors or spectators? Great and mean
Meet massed in death, who lends what life must borrow.
As long as skies are blue, and fields are green,
Evening must usher night, night urge the morrow,
Month follow month with woe, and year wake year to sorrow.

XXII

He will awake no more, oh, never more!
'Wake thou,' cried Misery, 'childless Mother, rise
Out of thy sleep, and slake, in thy heart's core,
A wound more fierce than his with tears and sighs.'
And all the Dreams that watched Urania's eyes,
And all the Echoes whom their sister's song
Had held in holy silence, cried: 'Arise!'
Swift as a Thought by the snake Memory stung,
From her ambrosial rest the fading Splendour sprung.

XXIII

She rose like an autumnal Night, that springs
Out of the East, and follows wild and drear
The golden Day, which, on eternal wings,
Even as a ghost abandoning a bier,
Had left the Earth a corpse. Sorrow and fear
So struck, so roused, so rapt Urania;
So saddened round her like an atmosphere
Of stormy mist; so swept her on her way
Even to the mournful place where Adonais lay.

XXIV

Our of her secret Paradise she sped,
Through camps and cities rough with stone, and steel,
And human hearts, which to her aery tread
Yielding not, wounded the invisible
Palms of her tender feet where'er they fell:
And barbèd tongues, and thoughts more sharp than they,
Rent the soft Form they never could repel,
Whose sacred blood, like the young tears of May,
Paved with eternal flowers that undeserving way.

XXV

In the death-chamber for a moment Death,
Shamed by the presence of that living Might,
Blushed to annihilation, and the breath
Revisited those lips, and Life's pale light
Flashed through those limbs, so late her dear delight.
'Leave me not wild and drear and comfortless,
As silent lightning leaves the starless night!
Leave me not!' cried Urania: her distress
Roused Death: Death rose and smiled, and met her vain caress.

XXVI

'Stay yet awhile! speak to me once again;
Kiss me, so long but as a kiss may live;
And in my heartless breast and burning brain
That word, that kiss, shall all thoughts else survive,
With food of saddest memory kept alive,
Now thou art dead, as if it were a part
Of thee, my Adonais! I would give
All that I am to be as thou now art!
But I am chained to Time, and cannot thence depart!

XXVII

'O gentle child, beautiful as thou wert,
Why didst thou leave the trodden paths of men
Too soon, and with weak hands though mighty heart
Dare the unpastured dragon in his den?
Defenceless as thou wert, oh, where was then
Wisdom the mirrored shield, or scorn the spear?
Or hadst thou waited the full cycle, when
Thy spirit should have filled its crescent sphere,
The monsters of life's waste had fled from thee like deer.

XXVIII

'The herded wolves, bold only to pursue;
The obscene ravens, clamorous o'er the dead;
The vultures to the conqueror's banner true
Who feed where Desolation first has fed,
And whose wings rain contagion;—how they fled,
When, like Apollo, from his golden bow
The Pythian of the age one arrow sped
And smiled!—The spoilers tempt no second blow,
They fawn on the proud feet that spurn them lying low.

XXIX

'The sun comes forth, and many reptiles spawn;
He sets, and each ephemeral insect then
Is gathered into death without a dawn,
And the immortal stars awake again;
So is it in the world of living men:
A godlike mind soars forth, in its delight
Making earth bare and veiling heaven, and when
It sinks, the swarms that dimmed or shared its light
Leave to its kindred lamps the spirit's awful night.'

XXX

Thus ceased she: and the mountain shepherds came,
Their garlands sere, their magic mantles rent;
The Pilgrim of Eternity, whose fame
Over his living head like Heaven is bent,
An early but enduring monument,
Came, veiling all the lightnings of his song
In sorrow; from her wilds Ierne sent
The sweetest lyrist of her saddest wrong,
And Love taught Grief to fall like music from his tongue.

XXXI

Midst others of less note, came one frail Form,
A phantom among men; companionless
As the last cloud of an expiring storm
Whose thunder is its knell; he, as I guess,
Had gazed on Nature's naked loveliness,
Actaeon-like, and now he fled astray
With feeble steps o'er the world's wilderness,
And his own thoughts, along that rugged way,
Pursued, like raging hounds, their father and their prey.

XXXII

A pardlike Spirit beautiful and swift—
A Love in desolation masked;—a Power
Girt round with weakness;—it can scarce uplift
The weight of the superincumbent hour;
It is a dying lamp, a falling shower,
A breaking billow;—even whilst we speak
Is it not broken? On the withering flower
The killing sun smiles brightly: on a cheek
The life can burn in blood, even while the heart may break.

XXXIII

His head was bound with pansies overblown,
And faded violets, white, and pied, and blue;
And a light spear topped with a cypress cone,
Round whose rude shaft dark ivy-tresses grew
Yet dripping with the forest's noonday dew,
Vibrated, as the ever-beating heart
Shook the weak hand that grasped it; of that crew
He came the last, neglected and apart;
A herd-abandoned deer struck by the hunter's dart.

XXXIV

All stood aloof, and at his partial moan
Smiled through their tears; well knew that gentle band
Who in another's fate now wept his own,
As in the accents of an unknown land
He sung new sorrow; sad Urania scanned
The Stranger's mien, and murmured: 'Who art thou?'
He answered not, but with a sudden hand
Made bare his branded and ensanguined brow,
Which was like Cain's or Christ's—oh! that it should be so!

XXXV

What softer voice is hushed over the dead?
Athwart what brow is that dark mantle thrown?
What form leans sadly o'er the white death-bed,
In mockery of monumental stone,
The heavy heart heaving without a moan?
If it be He, who, gentlest of the wise,
Taught, soothed, loved, honoured the departed one,
Let me not vex, with inharmonious sighs,
The silence of that heart's accepted sacrifice.

XXXVI

Our Adonais has drunk poison—oh!
What deaf and viperous murderer could crown
Life's early cup with such a draught of woe?
The nameless worm would now itself disown:
It felt, yet could escape, the magic tone
Whose prelude held all envy, hate, and wrong,
But what was howling in one breast alone,
Silent with expectation of the song,
Whose master's hand is cold, whose silver lyre unstrung.

XXXVII

Live thou, whose infamy is not thy fame!
Live! fear no heavier chastisement from me,
Thou noteless blot on a remembered name!
But be thyself, and know thyself to be!
And ever at thy season be thou free
To spill the venom when thy fangs o'erflow:
Remorse and Self-contempt shall cling to thee;
Hot Shame shall burn upon thy secret brow,
And like a beaten hound tremble thou shalt—as now.

XXXVIII

Nor let us weep that our delight is fled
Far from these carrion kites that scream below;
He wakes or sleeps with the enduring dead;
Thou canst not soar where he is sitting now—
Dust to the dust! but the pure spirit shall flow
Back to the burning fountain whence it came,
A portion of the Eternal, which must glow
Through time and change, unquenchably the same,
Whilst thy cold embers choke the sordid hearth of shame.

XXXIX

Peace, peace! he is not dead, he doth not sleep—
He hath awakened from the dream of life—
'Tis we, who lost in stormy visions, keep
With phantoms an unprofitable strife,
And in mad trance, strike with our spirit's knife
Invulnerable nothings.—*We* decay
Like corpses in a charnel; fear and grief
Convulse us and consume us day by day,
And cold hopes swarm like worms within our living clay.

XL

He has outsoared the shadow of our night;
Envy and calumny and hate and pain,
And that unrest which men miscall delight,
Can touch him not and torture not again;
From the contagion of the world's slow stain
He is secure, and now can never mourn
A heart grown cold, a head grown grey in vain;
Nor, when the spirit's self has ceased to burn,
With sparkless ashes load an unlamented urn.

XLI

He lives, he wakes—'tis Death is dead, not he;
Mourn not for Adonais.—Thou young Dawn,
Turn all thy dew to splendour, for from thee
The spirit thou lamentest is not gone;
Ye caverns and ye forests, cease to moan!
Cease, ye faint flowers and fountains, and thou Air,
Which like a mourning veil thy scarf hadst thrown
O'er the abandoned Earth, now leave it bare
Even to the joyous stars which smile on its despair!

XLII

He is made one with Nature: there is heard
His voice in all her music, from the moan
Of thunder, to the song of night's sweet bird;
He is a presence to be felt and known
In darkness and in light, from herb and stone,
Spreading itself where'er that Power may move
Which has withdrawn his being to its own;
Which wields the world with never-wearied love,
Sustains it from beneath, and kindles it above.

XLIII

He is a portion of the loveliness
Which once he made more lovely: he doth bear
His part, while the one Spirit's plastic stress
Sweeps through the dull dense world, compelling there
All new successions to the forms they wear;
Torturing th' unwilling dross that checks its flight
To its own likeness, as each mass may bear;
And bursting in its beauty and its might
From trees and beasts and men into the Heaven's light.

XLIV

The splendours of the firmament of time
May be eclipsed, but are extinguished not;
Like stars to their appointed height they climb,
And death is a low mist which cannot blot
The brightness it may veil. When lofty thought
Lifts a young heart above its mortal lair,
And love and life contend in it, for what
Shall be its earthly doom, the dead live there
And move like winds of light on dark and stormy air.

XLV

The inheritors of unfulfilled renown
Rose from their thrones, built beyond mortal thought,
Far in the Unapparent. Chatterton
Rose pale,—his solemn agony had not
Yet faded from him; Sidney, as he fought
And as he fell and as he lived and loved
Sublimely mild, a Spirit without spot,
Arose; and Lucan, by his death approved:
Oblivion as they rose shrank like a thing reproved.

XLVI

And many more, whose names on Earth are dark
But whose transmitted effluence cannot die
So long as fire outlives the parent spark,
Rose, robed in dazzling immortality.
'Thou art become as one of us,' they cry,
'It was for thee yon kingless sphere has long
Swung blind in unascended majesty,
Silent alone amid an Heaven of Song.
Assume thy wingèd throne, thou Vesper of our throng!'

XLVII

Who mourns for Adonais? Oh, come forth
Fond wretch! and know thyself and him aright.
Clasp with thy panting soul the pendulous Earth;
As from a centre, dart thy spirit's light
Beyond all worlds, until its spacious might
Satiate the void circumference: then shrink
Even to a point within our day and night;
And keep thy heart light lest it make thee sink
When hope has kindled hope, and lured thee to the brink.

XLVIII

Or go to Rome, which is the sepulchre,
Oh, not of him, but of our joy: 'tis nought
That ages, empires, and religions there
Lie buried in the ravage they have wrought;
For such as he can lend,—they borrow not
Glory from those who made the world their prey;
And he is gathered to the kings of thought
Who waged contention with their time's decay,
And of the past are all that cannot pass away.

XLIX

Go thou to Rome,—at once the Paradise,
The grave, the city, and the wilderness;
And where its wrecks like shattered mountains rise,
And flowering weeds, and fragrant copses dress
The bones of Desolation's nakedness
Pass, till the spirit of the spot shall lead
Thy footsteps to a slope of green access
Where, like an infant's smile, over the dead
A light of laughing flowers along the grass is spread;

L

And grey walls moulder round, on which dull Time
Feeds, like slow fire upon a hoary brand;
And one keen pyramid with wedge sublime,
Pavilioning the dust of him who planned
This refuge for his memory, doth stand
Like flame transformed to marble; and beneath,
A field is spread, on which a newer band
Have pitched in Heaven's smile their camp of death,
Welcoming him we lose with scarce extinguished breath.

LI

Here pause: these graves are all too young as yet
To have outgrown the sorrow which consigned
Its charge to each; and if the seal is set,
Here, on one fountain of a mourning mind,
Break it not thou! too surely shalt thou find
Thine own well full, if thou returnest home,
Of tears and gall. From the world's bitter wind
Seek shelter in the shadow of the tomb.
What Adonais is, why fear we to become?

LII

The One remains, the many change and pass;
Heaven's light forever shines, Earth's shadows fly;
Life, like a dome of many-coloured glass,
Stains the white radiance of Eternity,
Until Death tramples it to fragments.—Die,
If thou wouldst be with that which thou dost seek!
Follow where all is fled!—Rome's azure sky,
Flowers, ruins, statues, music, words, are weak
The glory they transfuse with fitting truth to speak.

LIII

Why linger, why turn back, why shrink, my Heart?
Thy hopes are gone before: from all things here
They have departed; thou shouldst now depart!
A light is passed from the revolving year,
And man, and woman; and what still is dear
Attracts to crush, repels to make thee wither.
The soft sky smiles,—the low wind whispers near:
'Tis Adonais calls! oh, hasten thither,
No more let Life divide what Death can join together.

LIV

That Light whose smile kindles the Universe,
That Beauty in which all things work and move,
That Benediction which the eclipsing Curse
Of birth can quench not, that sustaining Love
Which through the web of being blindly wove
By man and beast and earth and air and sea,
Burns bright or dim, as each are mirrors of
The fire for which all thirst; now beams on me,
Consuming the last clouds of cold mortality.

LV

The breath whose might I have invoked in song
Descends on me; my spirit's bark is driven
Far from the shore, far from the trembling throng
Whose sails were never to the tempest given;
The massy earth and spherèd skies are riven!
I am borne darkly, fearfully, afar;
Whilst, burning through the inmost veil of Heaven,
The soul of Adonais, like a star,
Beacons from the abode where the Eternal are.

Written on Hearing the News
of the Death of Napoleon

What! alive and so bold, O Earth?
   Art thou not overbold?
   What! leapest thou forth as of old
In the light of thy morning mirth,
The last of the flock of the starry fold?
Ha! leapest thou forth as of old?
Are not the limbs still when the ghost is fled,
And canst thou move, Napoleon being dead?

How! is not thy quick heart cold?
   What spark is alive on thy hearth?
How! is not *his* death-knell knolled?
   And livest *thou* still, Mother Earth?
Thou wert warming thy fingers old
O'er the embers covered and cold
Of that most fiery spirit, when it fled—
What, Mother, do you laugh now he is dead?

'Who has known me of old,' replied Earth,
   'Or who has my story told?
   It is thou who art overbold.'
And the lightning of scorn laughed forth
As she sung, 'To my bosom I fold
All my sons when their knell is knolled,
And so with living motion all are fed,
And the quick spring like weeds out of the dead.

'Still alive and still bold,' shouted Earth,
   'I grow bolder and still more bold.
   The dead fill me ten thousandfold
Fuller of speed, and splendour, and mirth.
I was cloudy, and sullen, and cold,
Like a frozen chaos uprolled,
Till by the spirit of the mighty dead
My heart grew warm. I feed on whom I fed.

'Ay, alive and still bold,' muttered Earth,
   'Napoleon's fierce spirit rolled,
   In terror and blood and gold,
A torrent of ruin to death from his birth.
Leave the millions who follow to mould
The metal before it be cold;
And weave into his shame, which like the dead
Shrouds me, the hopes that from his glory fled.'

When Passion's Trance is Overpast

When passion's trance is overpast,
If tenderness and truth could last,
Or live, whilst all wild feelings keep
Some mortal slumber, dark and deep,
I should not weep, I should not weep!

It were enough to feel, to see,
Thy soft eyes gazing tenderly,
And dream the rest—and burn and be
The secret food of fires unseen,
Couldst thou but be as thou hast been.

After the slumber of the year
The woodland violets reappear;
All things revive in field or grove,
And sky and sea, but two, which move
And form all others, life and love.

The Serpent is Shut Out from Paradise

The serpent is shut out from Paradise.
> The wounded deer must seek the herb no more
>   In which its heart-cure lies:
> The widowed dove must cease to haunt a bower
Like that from which its mate with feignèd sighs
>   Fled in the April hour.
> I too must seldom seek again
Near happy friends a mitigated pain.

II

Of hatred I am proud,—with scorn content;
> Indifference, which once hurt me, now is grown
>   Itself indifferent;
> But, not to speak of love, pity alone
Can break a spirit already more than bent.
>   The miserable one
> Turns the mind's poison into food,—
Its medicine is tears,—its evil good.

III

Therefore, if now I see you seldomer,
> Dear friends, dear *friend*! know that I only fly
>   Your looks, because they stir
> Griefs that should sleep, and hopes that cannot die:
The very comfort that they minister
>   I scarce can bear, yet I,
> So deeply is the arrow gone,
Should quickly perish if it were withdrawn.

IV

When I return to my cold home, you ask
    Why I am not as I have lately been.
        You spoil me for the task
Of acting a forced part in life's dull scene,—
    Of wearing on my brow the idle mask
        Of author, great or mean,
    In the world's carnival. I sought
Peace thus, and but in you I found it not.

V

Full half an hour, today, I tried my lot
    With various flowers, and every one still said,
        'She loves me—loves me not.'
    And if this meant a vision long since fled—
If it meant fortune, fame, or peace of thought—
        If it meant,—but I dread
    To speak what you may know too well:
Still there was truth in the sad oracle.

VI

The crane o'er seas and forests seeks her home;
    No bird so wild but has its quiet nest,
        When it no more would roam;
    The sleepless billows on the ocean's breast
Break like a bursting heart, and die in foam,
        And thus at length find rest:
    Doubtless there is a place of peace
Where *my* weak heart and all its throbs will cease.

VII

I asked her, yesterday, if she believed
    That I had resolution. One who *had*
        Would ne'er have thus relieved
    His heart with words,—but what his judgment bade
Would do, and leave the scorner unrelieved.
        These verses are too sad
    To send to you, but that I know,
Happy yourself, you feel another's woe.

To Jane: The Invitation

Best and brightest, come away!
Fairer far than this fair Day,
Which, like thee to those in sorrow,
Comes to bid a sweet good-morrow
To the rough Year just awake
In its cradle on the brake.
The brightest hour of unborn Spring,
Through the winter wandering,
Found, it seems, the halcyon Morn
To hoar February born.
Bending from Heaven, in azure mirth,
It kissed the forehead of the Earth,
And smiled upon the silent sea,
And bade the frozen streams be free,
And waked to music all their fountains,
And breathed upon the frozen mountains,
And like a prophetess of May
Strewed flowers upon the barren way,
Making the wintry world appear
Like one on whom thou smilest, dear.

Away, away, from men and towns,
To the wild wood and the downs—
To the silent wilderness
Where the soul need not repress
Its music lest it should not find
An echo in another's mind,
While the touch of Nature's art
Harmonizes heart to heart.
I leave this notice on my door
For each accustomed visitor:—
'I am gone into the fields
To take what this sweet hour yields;—
Reflection, you may come to-morrow;

Sit by the fireside with Sorrow.—
You with the unpaid bill, Despair,—
You, tiresome verse-reciter, Care,—
I will pay you in the grave,—
Death will listen to your stave.
Expectation too, be off!
Today is for itself enough;
Hope, in pity mock not Woe
With smiles, nor follow where I go;
Long having lived on your sweet food,
At length I find one moment's good
After long pain—with all your love,
This you never told me of.'

Radiant Sister of the Day,
Awake! arise! and come away!
To the wild woods and the plains,
And the pools where winter rains
Image all their roof of leaves,
Where the pine its garland weaves
Of sapless green and ivy dun
Round stems that never kiss the sun;
Where the lawns and pastures be,
And the sandhills of the sea;—
Where the melting hoar-frost wets
The daisy-star that never sets,
And wind-flowers, and violets,
Which yet join not scent to hue,
Crown the pale year weak and new;
When the night is left behind
In the deep east, dun and blind,
And the blue noon is over us,
And the multitudinous
Billows murmur at our feet,
Where the earth and ocean meet,
And all things seem only one
In the universal sun.

To Jane: The Recollection

Now the last day of many days,
    All beautiful and bright as thou,
      The loveliest and the last, is dead,
Rise, Memory, and write its praise!
    Up,—to thy wonted work! come, trace
      The epitaph of glory fled,—
For now the Earth has changed its face,
    A frown is on the Heaven's brow.

I

We wandered to the Pine Forest
    That skirts the Ocean's foam,
The lightest wind was in its nest,
    The Tempest in its home.
The whispering waves were half asleep,
    The clouds were gone to play,
And on the bosom of the deep
    The smile of Heaven lay;
It seemed as if the hour were one
    Sent from beyond the skies,
Which scattered from above the sun
    A light of Paradise.

II

We paused amid the pines that stood
    The giants of the waste,
Tortured by storms to shapes as rude
    As serpents interlaced,
And soothed by every azure breath,
    That under Heaven is blown,
To harmonies and hues beneath,
    As tender as its own;
Now all the tree-tops lay asleep,
    Like green waves on the sea,

As still as in the silent deep
   The ocean woods may be.

III

How calm it was!—the silence there
   By such a chain was bound
That even the busy woodpecker
   Made stiller by her sound
The inviolable quietness;
   The breath of peace we drew
With its soft motion made not less
   The calm that round us grew.
There seemed from the remotest seat
   Of the white mountain waste,
To the soft flower beneath our feet,
   A magic circle traced,—
A spirit interfused around
   A thrilling, silent life,—
To momentary peace it bound
   Our mortal nature's strife;
And still I felt the centre of
   The magic circle there
Was one fair form that filled with love
   The lifeless atmosphere.

IV

We paused beside the pools that lie
   Under the forest bough,—
Each seemed as 'twere a little sky
   Gulfed in a world below;
A firmament of purple light
   Which in the dark earth lay,
More boundless than the depth of night,
   And purer than the day—
In which the lovely forests grew,
   As in the upper air,
More perfect both in shape and hue

Than any spreading there.
There lay the glade and neighbouring lawn,
   And through the dark green wood
The white sun twinkling like the dawn
   Out of a speckled cloud.
Sweet views which in our world above
   Can never well be seen,
Were imaged by the water's love
   Of that fair forest green.
And all was interfused beneath
   With an Elysian glow,
An atmosphere without a breath,
   A softer day below.
Like one beloved the scene had lent
   To the dark water's breast,
Its every leaf and lineament
   With more than truth expressed;
Until an envious wind crept by,
   Like an unwelcome thought,
Which from the mind's too faithful eye
   Blots one dear image out.
Though thou art ever fair and kind,
   The forests ever green,
Less oft is peace in Shelley's mind,
   Than calm in waters, seen.

To Jane

The keen stars were twinkling,
And the fair moon was rising among them,
    Dear Jane!
The guitar was tinkling,
But the notes were not sweet till you sung them
    Again.
As the moon's soft splendour
O'er the faint cold starlight of Heaven
    Is thrown,
So your voice most tender
To the strings without soul had then given
    Its own.

The stars will awaken,
Though the moon sleep a full hour later,
    Tonight;
No leaf will be shaken
Whilst the dews of your melody scatter
    Delight.
Though the sound overpowers,
Sing again, with your dear voice revealing
    A tone
Of some world far from ours,
Where music and moonlight and feeling
    Are one.

Lines written in the Bay of Lerici

She left me at the silent time
When the moon had ceased to climb
The azure path of Heaven's steep,
And like an albatross asleep,
Balanced on her wings of light,
Hovered in the purple night,
Ere she sought her ocean nest
In the chambers of the West.
She left me, and I stayed alone
Thinking over every tone
Which, though now silent to the ear,
The enchanted heart could hear,
Like notes which die when born, but still
Haunt the echoes of the hill;
And feeling ever—oh, too much!—
The soft vibration of her touch,
As if her gentle hand, even now,
Lightly trembled on my brow;
And thus, although she absent were,
Memory gave me all of her
That even Fancy dares to claim:—
Her presence had made weak and tame
All passions, and I lived alone
In the time which is our own;
The past and future were forgot,
As they had been, and would be, not.
But soon, the guardian angel gone,
The daemon reassumed his throne
In my faint heart. I dare not speak
My thoughts, but thus disturbed and weak
I sat and watched the vessels glide
Over the ocean bright and wide,
Like spirit-wingèd chariots sent
O'er some serenest element

For ministrations strange and far;
As if to some Elysian star
Sailed for drink to medicine
Such sweet and bitter pain as mine.
And the wind that winged their flight
From the land came fresh and light,
And the scent of wingèd flowers,
And the coolness of the hours
Of dew, and sweet warmth left by day,
Were scattered o'er the twinkling bay.
And the fisher with his lamp
And spear about the low rocks damp
Crept, and struck the fish which came
To worship the delusive flame.
Too happy they, whose pleasure sought
Extinguishes all sense and thought
Of the regret that pleasure [   ]
Destroying life alone, not peace!

The Triumph of Life

Swift as a spirit hastening to his task
　　Of glory and of good, the sun sprang forth
Rejoicing in his splendour, and the mask

　　Of darkness fell from the awakened earth—
The smokeless altars of the mountain snows
　　Flamed above crimson clouds, and at the birth

Of light, the ocean's orison arose
　　To which the birds tempered their matin lay.
All flowers in field or forest which unclose

　　Their trembling eyelids to the kiss of day,
Swinging their censers in the element,
　　With orient incense lit by the new ray

Burned slow and inconsumably, and sent
　　Their odorous sighs up to the smiling air;
And, in succession due, did continent,

　　Isle, ocean, and all things that in them wear
The form and character of mortal mould,
　　Rise as the sun their father rose, to bear

Their portion of the toil, which he of old
　　Took as his own, and then imposed on them:
But I, whom thoughts which must remain untold

　　Had kept as wakeful as the stars that gem
The cone of night, now they were laid asleep
　　Stretched my faint limbs beneath the hoary stem

Which an old chestnut flung athwart the steep
　　Of a green Apennine: before me fled
The night; behind me rose the day; the deep

Was at my feet, and Heaven above my head,—
When a strange trance over my fancy grew
  Which was not slumber, for the shade it spread

Was so transparent, that the scene came through
  As clear as when a veil of light is drawn
O'er evening hills they glimmer; and I knew

That I had felt the freshness of that dawn,
Bathed in the same cold dew my brow and hair,
  And sate as thus upon that slope of lawn .

Under the self same bough, and heard as there
  The birds, the fountains and the ocean hold
Sweet talk in music through the enamoured air.
  And then a Vision on my brain was rolled. . .

As in that trance of wondrous thought I lay,
  This was the tenor of my waking dream:—
Methought I sate beside a public way

  Thick strewn with summer dust, and a great stream
Of people there was hurrying to and fro,
  Numerous as gnats upon the evening gleam,

All hastening onward, yet none seemed to know
  Whither he went, or whence he came, or why
He made one of the multitude, yet so

  Was borne amid the crowd, as through the sky
One of the million leaves of summer's bier;
  Old age and youth, manhood and infancy,

Mixed in one mighty torrent did appear,
  Some flying from the thing they feared, and some
Seeking the object of another's fear;

  And others, as with steps towards the tomb,
Pored on the trodden worms that crawled beneath,
  And others mournfully within the gloom

Of their own shadow walked, and called it death;
　　And some fled from it as it were a ghost,
　　Half fainting in the affliction of vain breath:

　　But more, with motions which each other crossed,
　　Pursued or shunned the shadows the clouds threw,
　　　Or birds within the noonday aether lost,

Upon that path where flowers never grew,—
　　And, weary with vain toil and faint for thirst,
　　Heard not the fountains, whose melodious dew

　　Out of their mossy cells forever burst;
　　Nor felt the breeze which from the forest told
　　　Of grassy paths and wood lawns interspersed

With overarching elms and caverns cold,
　　And violet banks where sweet dreams brood, but they
　　Pursued their serious folly as of old.

　　And as I gazed, methought that in the way
　　The throng grew wilder, as the woods of June
　　　When the south wind shakes the extinguished day,

And a cold glare, intenser than the noon,
　　But icy cold, obscured with [　] light
　　The sun, as he the stars. Like the young moon—

　　When on the sunlit limits of the night
　　Her white shell trembles amid crimson air,
　　　And whilst the sleeping tempest gathers might—

Doth, as a herald of its coming, bear
　　The ghost of her dead mother, whose dim form
　　Bends in dark aether from her infant's chair,—

　　So came a chariot on the silent storm
　　Of its own rushing splendour, and a Shape
　　　So sate within, as one whom years deform,

Beneath a dusky hood and double cape,
  Crouching within the shadow of a tomb;
And o'er what seemed the head, a cloud-like crape

  Was bent, a dun and faint aethereal gloom
Tempering the light. Upon the chariot beam
  A Janus-visaged Shadow did assume

The guidance of that wonder-wingèd team;
  The Shapes which drew it in thick lightnings
Were lost:—I heard alone on the air's soft stream

  The music of their ever-moving wings.
All the four faces of that Charioteer
  Had their eyes banded; little profit brings

Speed in the van and blindness in the rear,
  Nor then avail the beams that quench the sun,—
Or that with banded eyes could pierce the sphere

  Of all that is, has been or will be done;
So ill was the car guided—but it passed
  With solemn speed majestically on.

The crowd gave way, and I arose aghast,
  Or seemed to rise, so mighty was the trance,
And saw, like clouds upon the thunder blast,

  The million with fierce song and maniac dance
Raging around—such seemed the jubilee
  As when to greet some conqueror's advance

Imperial Rome poured forth her living sea
  From senate-house, and prison, and theatre
When Freedom left those who upon the free

  Had bound a yoke, which soon they stooped to bear.
Nor wanted here the true similitude
  Of a triumphal pageant, for where'er

The chariot rolled, a captive multitude
    Was driven;—all those who had grown old in power
Or misery,—all who have their age subdued

    By action or by suffering, and whose hour
Was drained to its last sand in weal or woe,
    So that the trunk survived both fruit and flower;—

All those whose fame or infamy must grow
    Till the great winter lay the form and name
Of their own earth with them forever low;—

    All but the sacred few who could not tame
Their spirits to the conqueror's—but as soon
    As they had touched the world with living flame,

Fled back like eagles to their native noon,
    Of those who put aside the diadem
Of earthly thrones or gems, till the last one

    Were there, for they of Athens or Jerusalem
Were neither mid the mighty captives seen,
    Nor mid the ribald crowd that followed them

Or fled before . . . Swift, fierce and obscene
    The wild dance maddens in the van, and those
Who lead it—fleet as shadows on the green,

    Outspeed the chariot, and without repose
Mix with each other in tempestuous measure
    To savage music, wilder as it grows,

They, tortured by the agonizing pleasure,
    Convulsed and on the rapid whirlwinds spun
Of that fierce Spirit, whose unholy leisure

    Was soothed by mischief since the world begun,
Throw back their heads and loose their streaming hair;
    And in their dance round her who dims the sun,

Maidens and youths fling their wild arms in air
 As their feet twinkle; they recede, and now
Bending within each other's atmosphere,

 Kindle invisibly—and as they glow,
Like moths by light attracted and repelled,
 Oft to new bright destruction come and go,

Till like two clouds into one vale impelled,
 That shake the mountains when their lightnings mingle
And die in rain—the fiery band which held

 Their natures, snaps—while the shock still may tingle;
One falls and then another in the path
 Senseless—nor is the desolation single,

Yet ere I can say *where*—the chariot hath
 Passed over them—nor other trace I find
But as of foam after the ocean's wrath

 Is spent upon the desert shore;—behind,
Old men, and women foully disarrayed,
 Shake their grey hair in the insulting wind,

Limp in the dance and strain with limbs decayed,
 Seeking to reach the light which leaves them still
Farther behind and deeper in the shade.

 But not the less with impotence of will
They wheel, though ghastly shadows interpose
 Round them and round each other, and fulfill

Their work, and to the dust from whence they rose
 Sink, and corruption veils them as they lie,
And frost in these performs what fire in those.

 Struck to the heart by this sad pageantry,
Half to myself I said—'And what is this?
 Whose shape is that within the car? And why—'

I would have added—'is all here amiss?—'
    But a voice answered—'Life!'—I turned and knew
(O Heaven, have mercy on such wretchedness!)

    That what I thought was an old root which grew
To strange distortion out of the hill side,
    Was indeed one of that deluded crew,

And that the grass, which methought hung so wide
    And white, was but his thin discoloured hair,
And that the holes it vainly sought to hide,

    Were or had been eyes:—'If thou canst, forbear
To join the dance, which I had well forborne!'
    Said the grim Feature (of my thought aware).

'I will now tell that which to this deep scorn
    Led me and my companions, and relate
The progress of the pageant since the morn;

    'If thirst of knowledge doth not thus abate,
Follow it even to the night, but I
    Am weary.'—Then like one who with the weight

Of his own words is staggered, wearily
    He paused; and ere he could resume, I cried:
'First, who art thou?'—'Before thy memory,

    'I feared, loved, hated, suffered, did, and died,
And if the spark with which Heaven lit my spirit
    Had been with purer nutriment supplied,

'Corruption would not now thus much inherit
    Of what was once Rousseau,—nor this disguise
Stain that within which still disdains to wear it;

    'If I have been extinguished, yet there rise
A thousand beacons from the spark I bore.'—
    'And who are those chained to the car?'—'The wise,

'The great, the unforgotten,—they who wore
Mitres and helms and crowns, or wreaths of light,
Signs of thought's empire over thought—their lore

'Taught them not this, to know themselves; their might
Could not repress the mutiny within,
And for the morn of truth they feigned, deep night

'Caught them ere evening.'—'Who is he with chin
Upon his breast and hands crossed on his chain?'—
'The child of a fierce hour; he sought to win

'The world, and lost all it did contain
Of greatness, in its hope destroyed; and more
Of fame and peace than virtue's self can gain

'Without the opportunity which bore
Him on its eagle pinions to the peak
From which a thousand climbers have before

'Fallen, as Napoleon fell.'—I felt my cheek
Alter to see the great form pass away,
Whose grasp had left the giant world so weak

That every pigmy kicked it as it lay;
And much I grieved to think how power and will
In opposition rule our mortal day,

And why God made irreconcilable
Good and the means of good; and for despair
I half disdained mine eyes' desire to fill

With the spent vision of the times that were
And scarce have ceased to be. —'Dost thou behold,'
Said then my guide, 'those spoilers spoiled, Voltaire,

'Frederick, and Kant, Catherine, and Leopold,
Chained hoary anarchs, demagogue and sage—
Whose names the fresh world thinks already old—

'For in the battle Life and they did wage,
    She remained conqueror. I was overcome
By my own heart alone, which neither age,

    'Nor tears, nor infamy, nor now the tomb
Could temper to its object.'—'Let them pass.'
    I cried, 'the world and its mysterious doom

'Is not so much more glorious than it was,
    That I desire to worship those who drew
New figures on its false and fragile glass

    'As the old faded.'—'Figures ever new
Rise on the bubble, paint them as you may;
    We have but thrown, as those before us threw,

'Our shadows on it as it passed away.
    But mark now chained to the triumphal chair
The mighty phantoms of an elder day;

    'All that is mortal of great Plato there
Expiates the joy and woe his master knew not;
    That star that ruled his doom was far too fair.

'And life, where long that flower of Heaven grew not,
    Conquered that heart by love, which gold or pain,
Or age, or sloth, or slavery could subdue not.

    'And near [   ] walk the [   ] twain,
The tutor and his pupil, whom Dominion
    Followed as tame as vulture in a chain.

'The world was darkened beneath either pinion
    Of him whom from the flock of conquerors
Fame singled as her thunder-bearing minion;

    'The other long outlived both woes and wars,
Throned in new thoughts of men, and still had kept
    The jealous keys of truth's eternal doors,

'If Bacon's spirit [   ] had not leapt
  Like lightning out of darkness—he compelled
The Proteus shape of Nature's, as it slept

  'To wake, and to unbar the caves that held
The treasure of the secrets of its reign.
  See the great bards of old who inly quelled

'The passions which they sung, as by their strain
  May well be known: their living melody
Tempers its own contagion to the vein

  'Of those who are infected with it—I
Have suffered what I wrote, or viler pain!

  'And so my words were seeds of misery—
Even as the deeds of others.'—'Not as theirs,'
  I said—he pointed to a company

In which I recognized amid the heirs
  Of Caesar's crime, from him to Constantine;
The anarchs old whose force and murderous snares

  Had founded many a sceptre-bearing line
And spread the plague of blood and gold abroad:
  And Gregory, and John, and men divine

Who rose like shadows between Man and god;
  Till that eclipse, still hanging under heaven,
Was worshipped by the world o'er which they strode,

  For the true sun it quenched.—'Their power was given
But to destroy,' replied the leader:—'I
  Am one of those who have created, even

'If it be but a world of agony.'—
  'Whence camest thou? and whither goest thou?
How did thy course begin?' I said, 'and why?

'Mine eyes are sick of this perpetual flow
Of people, and my heart of one sad thought—
    Speak!'—'Whence I came, partly I seem to know,

'And how and by what paths I have been brought
    To this dread pass, methinks even thou mayst guess;—
Why this should be, my mind can compass not;

'Whither the conqueror hurries me, still less;—
But follow thou, and from spectator turn
    Actor or victim in this wretchedness,

'And what thou wouldst be taught I then may learn
    From thee. Now listen: — In the April prime,
When all the forest-tips began to burn

'With kindling green, touched by the azure clime
Of the young season, I found myself asleep
    Under a mountain, which from unknown time

'Had yawned into a cavern, high and deep;
    And from it came a gentle rivulet,
Whose water, like clear air, in its calm sweep

'Bent the soft grass, and kept for ever wet
The stems of the sweet flowers, and filled the grove
    With sounds, which all who hear must needs forget

'All pleasure and all pain, all hate and love,
    Which they had known before that hour of rest;
A sleeping mother then would dream not of

'The only child who died upon her breast
At eventide—a king would mourn no more
    The crown of which his brow was dispossesed

'When the sun lingered o'er the ocean floor
    To gild his rival's new prosperity.
Thou wouldst forget thus vainly to deplore

'Ills, which if ills can find no cure from thee,
The thought of which no other sleep will quell,
    Nor other music blot from memory,

'So sweet and deep is the oblivious spell;
    Whether my life had been before that sleep
The Heaven which I imagine, or a Hell

'Like this harsh world in which I wake to weep,
I know not. I arose, and for a space
    The scene of woods and waters seemed to keep,

'Though it was now broad day, a gentle trace
    Of light diviner than the common sun
Sheds on the common earth, but all the place

'Was filled with many sounds woven into one
Oblivious melody, confusing sense
    Amid the gliding waves and shadows dun;

'And, as I looked, the bright omnipresence
    Of morning through the orient cavern flowed,
And the sun's image radiantly intense

'Burned on the waters of the well that glowed
Like gold, and threaded all the forest maze
    With winding paths of emerald fire; there stood

'Amid the sun, as he amid the blaze
    Of his own glory, on the vibrating
Floor of the fountain, paved with flashing rays,

'A Shape all light, which with one hand did fling
Dew on the earth, as if she were the dawn
    Whose invisible rain forever seemed to sing

'A silver music on the mossy lawn;
    And still before her on the dusky grass,
Iris her many-coloured scarf had drawn:

'In her right hand she bore a crystal glass
Mantling with bright Nepenthe; the fierce splendour
   Fell from her as she moved under the mass

'Of the deep cavern, and with palms so tender,
   Their tread broke not the mirror of its billow,
Glided along the river, and did bend her

'Head under the dark boughs, till like a willow
Her fair hair swept the bosom of the stream
   That whispered with delight to be their pillow.

'As one enamoured is upborne in dream
   O'er lily-paven lakes, mid silver mist,
To wondrous music, so this Shape might seem

'Partly to tread the waves with feet which kissed
The dancing foam; partly to glide along
   The airs that roughened the moist amethyst,

'Or the faint morning beams that fell among
   The trees, or the soft shadows of the trees;
And her feet, ever to the ceaseless song

'Of leaves, and winds, and waves, and birds, and bees,
And falling drops, moved in a measure new
   Yet sweet, as on the summer evening breeze,

'Up from the lake a shape of golden dew
   Between two rocks, athwart the rising moon,
Dances i' the wind, where never eagle flew;

'And still her feet, no less than the sweet tune
To which they moved, seemed as they moved to blot
   The thoughts of him who gazed on them; and soon

'All that was, seemed as if it had been not;
   As if the gazer's mind was strewn beneath
Her feet like embers; and she, thought by thought,

'Trampled its fires into the dust of death;
As day upon the threshold of the east
    Treads out the lamps of night, until the breath

'Of darkness re-illumine even the least
    Of heaven's living eyes—like day she came,
Making the night a dream; and ere she ceased

'To move, as one between desire and shame
Suspended, I said—If, as it doth seem,
    Thou comest from the realm without a name

'Into this valley of perpetual dream,
    Shew whence I came, and where I am, and why—
Pass not away upon the passing stream.

'Arise and quench thy thirst, was her reply.
And as a shut lily, stricken by the wand
    Of dewy morning's vital alchemy,

I rose; and, bending at her sweet command,
    Touched with faint lips the cup she raised,
And suddenly my brain became as sand

'Where the first wave had more than half erased
The track of deer on desert Labrador;
    Whilst the wolf, from which they fled amazed,

'Leaves his stamp visibly upon the shore,
    Until the second bursts;—so on my sight
Burst a new Vision, never seen before,

'And the fair shape waned in the coming light,
As veil by veil the silent splendour drops
    From Lucifer, amid the chrysolite

'Of sunrise, ere it strike the mountain-tops;
    And as the presence of that fairest planet,
Although unseen, is felt by one who hopes

'That his day's path may end as he began it,
In that star's smile, whose light is like the scent
  Of a jonquil when evening breezes fan it,

'Or the soft note in which his dear lament
  The Brescian shepherd breathes, or the caress
That turned his weary slumber to content;

  'So knew I in that light's severe excess
The presence of that Shape which on the stream
  Moved, as I moved along the wilderness,

'More dimly than a day-appearing dream,
  The ghost of a forgotten form of sleep;
A light from Heaven, whose half-extinguished beam

  'Through the sick day in which we wake to weep
Glimmers, forever sought, forever lost;
  So did that shape its obscure tenor keep

'Beside my path, as silent as a ghost;
  But the new Vision, and its cold bright car,
With savage music, stunning music, crossed

  'The forest, and as if from some dread war
Triumphantly returning, the loud million
  Fiercely extolled the fortune of her star.

'A moving arch of victory, the vermilion
  And green and azure plumes of Iris had
Built high over her wind-wingèd pavilion,

  'And underneath aethereal glory clad
The wilderness, and far before her flew
  The tempest of the splendour, which forbade

'Shadow to fall from leaf or stone; the crew
  Seemed in that light like atomies that dance
Within a sunbeam;—some upon the new

'Embroidery of flowers, that did enhance
The grassy vesture of the desert, played,
    Forgetful of the chariot's swift advance;

'Others stood gazing, till within the shade
    Of the great mountain its light left them dim;
Others outspeeded it; and others made

    'Circles around it, like the clouds that swim
Round the high moon in a bright sea of air;
    And more did follow, with exulting hymn,

'The chariot and the captives fettered there:—
    But all like bubbles on an eddying flood
Fell into the same track at last, and were

    'Borne onward.—I among the multitude
Was swept—me, sweetest flowers delayed not long;
    Me, not the shadow nor the solitude;

'Me, not the falling stream's Lethean song;
    Me, not the phantom of that early Form
Which moved upon its motion—but among

    'The thickest billows of the living storm
I plunged, and bared my bosom to the clime
    Of that cold light, whose airs too soon deform.

'Before the chariot had begun to climb
    The opposing steep of that mysterious dell,
Behold a wonder worthy of the rhyme

    'Of him whom from the lowest depths of Hell,
Through every Paradise and through all glory,
    Love led serene, and who returned to tell

'The words of hate and awe; the wondrous story
    How all things are transfigured except Love;
For deaf as is a sea, which wrath makes hoary,

'The world can hear not the sweet notes that move
The sphere whose light is melody to lovers—
     A wonder worthy of his rhyme.—The grove

'Grew dense with shadows to its inmost covers,
     The earth was grey with phantoms, and the air
Was peopled with dim forms, as when there hovers

     'A flock of vampire-bats before the glare
Of the tropic sun, bringing, ere evening,
     Strange night upon some Indian isle;—thus were

'Phantoms diffused around, and some did fling
     Shadows of shadows, yet unlike themselves,
Behind them; some like eaglets on the wing

     'Were lost in the white blaze; others like elves
Danced in a thousand unimagined shapes
     Upon the sunny streams and grassy shelves;

'And others sate chattering like restless apes
     On vulgar hands and voluble like fire;
Some made a cradle of the ermined capes

     'Of kingly mantles; some upon the tiar
Of pontiffs sate like vultures; others played
     Within the crown which girt with empire

'A baby's or an idiot's brow, and made
     Their nests in it. The old anatomies
Sate hatching their bare broods under the shade

     'Of daemon wings, and laughed from their dead eyes
To reassume the delegated power,
     Arrayed in which these worms did monarchize,

'Who make this earth their charnel. Others more
     Humble, like falcons, sate upon the fist
Of common men, and round their heads did soar;

'Or like small gnats and flies, as thick as mist
On evening marshes, thronged about the brow
   Of lawyer, statesman, priest and theorist;—

'And others, like discoloured flakes of snow
   On fairest bosoms and the sunniest hair,
Fell, and were melted by the youthful glow

'Which they extinguished; and, like tears, they were
A veil to those from whose faint lids they rained
   In drops of sorrow. I became aware

'Of whence those forms proceeded which thus stained
   The track in which we moved. After brief space,
From every form the beauty slowly waned;

'From every firmest limb and fairest face
The strength and freshness fell like dust, and left
   The action and the shape without the grace

'Of life. The marble brow of youth was cleft
   With care; and in the eyes where once hope shone,
Desire, like a lioness bereft

'Of its last cub, glared ere it died; each one
Of that great crowd sent forth incessantly
   These shadows, numerous as the dead leaves blown

'In autumn evening from a poplar tree.
   Each like himself and like each other were
At first; but some distorted seemed to be

'Obscure clouds, moulded by the casual air;
And of this stuff the car's creative ray
   Wrought all the busy phantoms that were there,

'As the sun shapes the clouds; thus on the way
   Mask after mask fell from the countenance
And form of all; and long before the day

'Was old, the joy which waked like Heaven's glance
The sleepers in the oblivious valley, died;
  And some grew weary of the ghastly dance,

'And fell, as I have fallen, by the wayside;—
  Those soonest from whose forms most shadows passed,
And least of strength and beauty did abide.'

  'Then, what is Life?' I said . . . the cripple cast
His eye upon the car which now had rolled
  Onward, as if that look must be the last,

And answered . . . 'Happy those for whom the fold
  Of

Minister—Love Thyself!

Sustaining Healthy Ministry

Chris Edmondson

Vicar of St Peter's, Shipley
Diocese of Bradford

GROVE BOOKS LIMITED
RIDLEY HALL RD CAMBRIDGE CB3 9HU

Contents

Acknowledgements

I would like to thank the members of the Grove Pastoral Group for their encouragement and advice in the production of this booklet; also those mentioned in the booklet who gave so willingly to me of their time and insights.

Finally, thanks are due to Andrée Freeman who typed the manuscript and Peter Hall who designed the cover picture. They are both members of St Peter's, Shipley, the church where I am vicar, whose PCC and congregation actively encourage its clergy to put into practice all that I advocate in this booklet!

The Cover Illustration is by Peter Hall

First Impression September 2000
ISSN 0144-171X
ISBN 1 85174 442 8

1

Introduction

'The Christian church is dying in the West...The Western church is not facing incomprehension or opposition so much as a massive indifference...It is the form of the church in the West which has become the biggest barrier to the gospel.'[1]

These comments, and many more like them, are part of a painfully realistic analysis of the situation in which churches and their leaders find themselves at the start of a new millennium. The writer Michael Riddell, to be fair, goes on to give some pointers of hope for the future, but the reality is we (and by this I mean the church in all its different expressions) are a church 'in transition.' Never before has the church faced operating in a post-Christian (or at least post-Christendom) culture, so we are becoming once more a 'missionary' church.

Clearly, it is not sufficient to offer 'more of the same' in terms of being church. Perhaps we hope that one day people will come to their senses and see that in and through that church and its gospel message they can find hope and meaning in life. It is this (albeit understandable) 'head in the sand' attitude, 'wishing things could be like they once were,' that has in fact contributed to the scenario that Riddell so radically exposes.

Whether we like it or not, and whether or not we recognize it and choose to call it by its 'catch-all' name—'postmodernity'—those who are leaders of the church and all its members are affected by the constantly changing scene that the term attempts to define.

So we face changes in world views, values, attitudes to institutions, social and political structures and much more besides. We are all caught up in this, and it is important to see it is not all negative, as if all that is emerging is 'the enemy.' However, we must learn to read the signs of the times. There are pressures and demands that have not been encountered before, but there are also exciting opportunities to be grasped. Spirituality is on the agenda again but as one writer has put it 'spirituality is alive and well but of no fixed abode.' There is a task to be done in connecting or re-connecting people with the One who is the end of all our searching, the God and Father of our Lord Jesus Christ. The problem is that for most people the church is irrelevant in this spiritual search, just one of the institutions of which we are suspicious.

What follows is an attempt to examine something of the context in which the church is called to worship and witness, and what resources and support clergy need to be effective in their leadership roles in this postmodern, consumerist, market-driven age.

If the question comes 'Why the emphasis on the clergy?' I hope you will soon

---

1   Michael Riddell, *Threshold of the Future* (London: SPCK, 1998) pp 29, 39.

discover that this is not at the expense of a total commitment to collaborative ministry. The fact is however that *'clergy are their [the denominations] most costly and essential investment.'*[2] The churches invest large sums of money in their education and initial training but often, after ordination or its equivalent, both training and support is patchy. I believe this contributes to the fact that clergy morale often seems to be low.

Low morale is also affected by the changing spiritual 'climate' and further compounded by the fact that in most of the mainstream denominations, clergy numbers have declined year on year. For example, in the Diocese of Hereford, in 1969 there were 300 stipendiary clergy, whereas in 1999 there were 121. Other dioceses would show similar figures, and are having to cut numbers to fit the 'Sheffield formula' (a system in the Church of England attempting to ensure a fairer distribution of clergy across the country). In the Anglican context very recently numbers of candidates going to selection conferences has gone up. This will, however, still not compensate for earlier decline and current retirement rates. On the positive side, a fresh vision has emerged for seizing this as an opportunity to restore ministry to the whole people of God, using lay people in new ways, but pressures, demands and uncertainties remain on the existing clergy and their role in such a transition period.

A further important reason for focussing on the clergy's role in this changing context is the issue of identity. Like other professions, the authority of the clergy is questioned in today's climate. But unlike (for example) doctors or teachers, clergy representing the church are not seen as essential to the make-up and survival of society. Furthermore, unlike most other professions, clergy are involved in their environment in an all-consuming way, often living 'over the shop' and not having clearly defined hours of work.

To illustrate this point further, note the order in Michael Moynagh's list of 'people to be trusted'[3] : Local doctor; Kelloggs; Cadbury's; Heinz; Nescafé; Rowntree; Bank; Coca Cola; *Church;* Police; MP. This shows starkly the extent of the market-driven/consumer age in which we find ourselves. As Moynagh goes on to suggest, whether we like it or not the Church of England is a type of brand, other denominations or streams being different brands. If that is people's perception, is it feasible for clergy to find an appropriate identity that is more than 'managing a brand'? Surely their calling is a higher and more significant one than that? To answer in the affirmative has implications in terms of training and support. However, before we explore what that might mean, we must first look a little more at the unfamiliar territory in which we find ourselves, and from which we dare not draw back in search of some elusive, long-gone safety. I end this section as I began, with a quotation from Michael Riddell: 'The new millennium is a time for irresponsible boldness.'[4]

2   Andrew R Irvine, *Between Two Worlds* (London: Mowbray, 1997) p 163.
3   Michael Moynagh, 'Church 2020—What will it be like?' in *RUN* magazine (Aylesbury: Spring 1999) p 9.
4   Riddell, *Threshold of the Future*, p 117.

2

A Changing Church in a Changing World

The origins of this piece of work were in a conversation with my spiritual director as to how I should best use the sabbatical I had been granted in the summer of 1999. I had been ordained then for 26 years and had worked in three different dioceses, representing a number of different contexts—urban, suburban and rural. In all three dioceses I had also had various diocesan responsibilities in the areas of mission, evangelism and pastoral strategy, so my spiritual director knew something of my passion to see the Church engaging appropriately with this fast-changing world.

Mind the Gap

In Numbers 16.47, in the context of a rebellion against Moses' authority, we find the curious phrase whereby Aaron is called to 'stand in the gap' between the living and the dead, and when he does so the plague affecting the people stops. It seems to me that part of the challenge and confusion facing ordained leadership today is identifying what these gaps are and where we are to stand!

We know that the gap between the church and the majority of the community is getting wider and deeper daily. But we are aware of other gaps that also impinge on our task—between generations, the 'haves' and 'have nots,' and those created by technology. It can feel overwhelming to try and address these at a personal level, never mind as a leader of a local church community. In a world where the postmodern view is summed up in the phrase: 'This is my truth; tell me yours,' [5] is it possible to present the Christian faith as an abiding truth rather than just another opinion, and if so, how?

Grace Davie in her book *Religion in Britain since 1945*[6] has described how 2/3 to 3/4 of the British public believe in some sort of God, but it is variously expressed in terms of 'privatized religion,' 'invisible religion,' 'implicit religion,' 'folk religion,' 'civic religion.' Hence yet another ever-widening gap between believing and belonging appears. The church, as seen in the survey in my Introduction, is low down on the list of institutions to be trusted, because in a postmodern society trust is built on relationships, not authority and institution.

Up until the mid-20th century, there was a sense of commitment to, or at least respect for, the church as one of society's institutions and thereby also respect for its clergy. Since the 1960s, various movements have challenged that, as the place of the individual has been asserted and personal freedom and choice reigns.

It seems to me that in the light of all this, 'standing in the gap' involves a reassessment and maybe even a rejection of what society thinks the role of the

5   Album title—Manic Street Preachers, Sony, 1998.
6   Grace Davie, *Religion in Britain Since 1945* (Oxford: Blackwell, 1994).

clergy is—as either irrelevant or as some kind of custodians of moral order. We need a fresh reflection on what we as clergy believe our role to be and maybe a challenge as to what congregations insist we should be and do. We will require help for this, to learn to hold in tension the 'inherited' and 'emerging' church (to use Robert Warren's phrase[7]) and to 'broker communication across the culture gap.'[8] J V Taylor coined the phrase 'the Go-between God'[9]; we also need 'go-between leaders.' It will be a vulnerable place, a tough assignment, but standing on the edges or at a distance is surely a denial of faith in an incarnate Lord.

A Local Focus

What follows is an attempt to explore how clergy can be resourced to grapple with some of these complex challenges and how they can help themselves.

To aid my researches I have visited or contacted a number of dioceses to see what might be common ground, and where particular geographical, sociological or demographic contexts make a difference. So, for example, Hereford ranks as the most sparsely populated diocese in the country. From my conversations there it seems that sparseness heightens commitment, with Hereford coming top of all the indicators of 'church strength' in terms of numbers baptized, confirmed and electoral roll members per head of population. Morale among clergy was said to be relatively high—due to a number of factors, among which were noted:

- quality of commitment to church life, as expressed in the above statistics;
- a pleasant area in which to live and minister;
- delayed appearance of the negative effects of postmodernity in a rural area;
- the historical importance of Celtic spirituality, making connection with people's current spiritual searching easier.

In Guildford Diocese, the bishop expressed a similar vision of the church being a 'catalytic agency' to reconnect people's spiritual openness with the gospel. But in other ways, the context for ministry and church life there is radically different. This diocese includes some of the most prosperous areas of the country, marked by the pressure to achieve and a frenetic activism. And it raises other issues. How can the church be counter-cultural and not be driven into activist mode? Non-work time is at a premium so where do the volunteers come from? Surrounded by considerable wealth, how can the clergy cope financially or deal with the general social expectations? Congregations' expectations of clergy are also very high.

In addition to meeting bishops from these two dioceses, I interviewed either members of the senior staff, CME (Continuing Ministerial Education) officers or their equivalents in the dioceses of Blackburn, Lichfield, Worcester and Rochester. I am grateful to them for their time and openness in exploring both the general picture and specific local implications.

---

7   See Robert Warren, *Being Human, Being Church* (London: Marshall Pickering, 1995).
8   Gerard Kelly, *Get a Grip on the Future Without Losing your Hold on the Past* (London: Monarch, 1999) p 236.
9   See J V Taylor, *The Go-between God* (London: Hodder and Stoughton, 1973).

3
Values and Skills

In his fascinating account of the vision for and establishment of the London Light-house, a hospice and centre for Aids patients, Christopher Spence, its first Director, writes about key values for the staff, paid and voluntary.[10] These include a right to good training, a right to personal development and a right to personal support. Christopher is now Chief Executive of The National Council for Volunteering, and in conversation with him about both organizations, it became clear how much the church can and needs to learn from the values evident in both. He spoke of the way in which people think and act best when they feel valued and of how we continually need new experience to face changing situations. Because much of the work of clergy takes us to the 'edges of life' there is a need here too for pastoral and emotional support. Sadly, in my experience, the church which should be in the forefront of modelling such values is often way behind.

Whilst well-defined structures are important, so that clergy are adequately resourced in skills and offered appropriate pastoral support, of equal importance is the quality of life in the organization—in this instance the Church, whether at national or diocesan level. We need to create a climate where people are valued and treated seriously. As the Bishop of Doncaster, Cyril Ashton, put it to me when he was working as Director of Training in Blackburn Diocese: 'Courses are important, but so are friendship, hospitality and generosity. We need to beware of making more demands—rather, we are in the business of offering resources.'

Establishing a Thinking Environment

A particular resource which picks up on embracing these kinds of values is Nancy Kline's work on establishing a 'thinking environment.' I believe that to put into practice some of these insights could literally be life-changing. Kline is a management consultant and the phrase comes from work which she has developed over 15 years and has described in her book *Time to Think*.[11] Her basic thesis, which sounds deceptively simple, is as follows:
- Everything we do depends for its quality on the thinking we do first. Our thinking depends on the quality of our *attention* for each other.
- A 'Thinking Environment' is a set of 10 conditions under which human beings can *think for themselves*—with rigour, imagination, courage and grace.[12] They are:
1. *Attention*   – listening with respect, interest and fascination
2. *Incisive Questions* – removing assumptions that limit ideas

---

10   See Christopher Spence, *On Watch* (London: Cassell, 1996).
11   Nancy Kline, *Time to Think* (London: Ward Lock, 1999).
12   *ibid*, p 13.

3. *Equality*	– treating each other as thinking peers
	– giving equal turns and attention
	– keeping agreements and boundaries
4. *Appreciation*	– practising a five-to-one ratio of appreciation to criticism
5. *Ease*	– offering freedom from rush or urgency
6. *Encouragement*	– moving beyond competition
7. *Feelings*	– allowing sufficient emotional release to restore thinking
8. *Information*	– providing a full and accurate picture of reality
9. *Place*	– creating a physical environment that says to people: 'you matter'
10. *Diversity*	– adding quality because of the differences between us

Kline's book describes how these principles can be related to every area of life and work—teams, meetings, supervision, peer mentoring, leadership, family.

Just look at the 10 conditions again and ask yourself 'Wouldn't it be wonderful for once to be listened to without interruption?' 'Wouldn't it be great to be part of an organization that offered more appreciation than criticism?' 'Wouldn't it be wonderful to know that those responsible for me and my family's welfare care about the house I live in?' I believe if those in ministry were on the receiving end of such support, it could transform their lives and enable them to offer better support to those in their care.

Reading Kline's book not only made me question how I myself treat and handle others, but also should not these qualities be what the 'structures' of the Church should provide for its clergy? This would necessitate appropriate training for bishops, archdeacons, CME officers and others in 'line management'—but if this was modelled by them, what a difference it could make to the morale of clergy and therefore to their parishioners. To quote Kline again: 'Such a thinking environment is natural but rare. It has been squeezed out of our lives and organizations by inferior ways of treating each other. Organizations, families and relationships can become thinking environments again, where good ideas abound, actions follow and *people flourish* (emphasis mine).'[13]

Skills Resourcing

All this highlights a number of key skills areas which need to be addressed:

Managing Volunteers

One of the key needs is to recruit and manage volunteers. In my experience this has had little attention, yet clergy spend much of their time on it. Bill Hybels, Senior Pastor of the Willowcreek Community Church in Chicago, describes the church as a 'volunteer intensive organization.'[14] Jesus started and built it that way through the call of his first disciples and this is how it continues.

---

13 Nancy Kline, *Time to Think*, p 13.
14 Heard at the Willowcreek Leaders' Conference in 1997.

Not only the church, but many other voluntary organizations, societies, political parties and trades unions are having problems with volunteering. At one time, particularly in more middle-class areas, there was a cultural expectation that working as a volunteer was 'something you do,' part of being a responsible citizen and member of the community. Now, the stresses and demands of work mean less time is available for such activity. Furthermore for young people, who might have taken a 'gap year' and worked as a volunteer, there are now more pressures to get quickly into the job market—not least to pay off university debts. Also, they are more sophisticated about what resonates as being worthwhile, or is seen to be 'cool'—and often the church does not figure too highly on that scale! Add to this the 'pic 'n' mix' approach to life that means long-term commitment to anything is less likely, volunteering being just one amongst other options available, and it is no wonder we struggle to recruit.

So how can we address this? I would suggest thinking needs to be done in the following areas:

i) Being creative as an organization about the language we use. The NCV (National Council for Volunteering) strapline for recruiting young people in the Millennium year was 'Build on what you're into'—seeing volunteering as an extension of what people are committed to and doing anyway, rather than as an 'add-on.'

ii) Learning to see and promote volunteering as an 'exchange' relationship—the church benefits but there are clear benefits to the volunteers themselves. It is not one-way traffic.

iii) Ensuring that commensurate support is given to match the expectations we have of volunteers. So often this is the reason people will not volunteer— firstly, they fear it will prove to be a 'life sentence' and secondly they think it is 'sink or swim.' Often, the person asking for volunteers is just pleased to have filled a gap and they move on to sort out the next problem, whereas to honour and value people means treating them seriously in terms of their support and ongoing training and having regular meetings with them.

iv) Having clear job descriptions for volunteers, in the same way we do for paid staff like curates, youth workers, administrators. These should be reviewed each year. This is about dignifying people and their work.

v) There is a need to avoid soft-pedalling in terms of what is expected of volunteers, but equally not to make undue or unrealistic demands either.

More training and resources are needed in this area. If we are committed to collaborative ministry we have to learn how to harness people's willingness and gifting. This includes, among other things, sensitivity in how we approach people new to the church community. Desperate for resources, new members have often been dragooned into areas of ministry for which they are neither suitable nor gifted. It is as people become part of the community that various strategies for discerning gifts can be put into place, for example by means of some kind of 'gift awareness' course.

There may also be more imaginative ways of making needs known. Recently, in the church where I am vicar, we have discovered from the various groups and organizations where the needs and gaps are. From there, we will create a 'Situations Vacant' board that indicates the nature of the work, how much time commitment is required and what support and training is available. (Obviously there are certain areas such as the healing ministry where we would approach things differently).

Along with this, the affirming and supporting of people in their lives as Christians 'in the world' is key. God's work is not just 'church' in the narrow gathered sense. We are called to be a church in dispersion and people deserve support and understanding in this too.

Teamwork/Collaborative Ministry

In the changing environment in which clergy are called to minister, where professional expectations are getting higher and where more is demanded of those in ministry, there needs to be continual assessment of training requirements and feedback to theological educators of what is required. The last 20 years have seen a healthy shift away from the omnicompetent, individualist approach that characterized much earlier training and its outworking in pastoral ministry. But for those trained in such models, it can come hard to 'learn new tricks' and even for those committed to a collaborative, teamwork approach I suspect there needs to be a re-training and re-equipping every few years.

In reality, of course, the concept of teamwork and collaboration is nothing new—rather, we are rediscovering something. So, for example, St Paul gives an extended meditation on the nature of the church as the body of Christ:

> 'The body is a unit...so it is with Christ...for we were all baptized by one Spirit into one body...now you are the body of Christ and each one of you is a part of it.' (1 Corinthians 12.12–31)

As St Paul makes clear, for the church to be effective, true to itself and its calling, all must work together for the good of the whole, using their God-given gifts. The role of the clergy as leaders of such collaborative ministry is vital—because, contrary to some views of collaborative ministry, the laity are not there to help the clergy to do their job. *The clergy are there to help the laity be the church.* Helping people to understand what this might mean in a changing environment is a key part of what continuing ministerial education needs to offer.

4

How Clergy are Supported

If there are all these emerging demands on our skills, then we also need appropriate support.

Appropriate CME

The phrase 'Continuing Ministerial Education' would, I suspect, have caused blank looks from earlier generations of clergy. You went to theological college, usually endured rather than enjoyed 'Post-Ordination Training' as a curate for three or four years and were thereby set up for a lifetime's ministry! The author Gerard Kelly challenges such an expectation now:

'In a static culture it is enough to learn skills once, perhaps in college, and to dedicate a life to practising them. In a culture re-inventing itself every five to seven years this is untenable…To be a leader in the coming decades will mean by definition to be a life-long learner.'[15]

Although there may still be a residue of the earlier attitudes around, there are some signs of hope, where the importance of a commitment to life-long learning as we respond to this changing context for ministry is being recognized. Evidence of this is seen in practical terms in the way most dioceses allocate a sum of money from their budgets for CME, varying between £100—£200 per clergyperson each year.

Not surprisingly, in the Church of England, there is no consistent approach to CME. However, it is possible to identify two overall but contrasting approaches—one *proactive*, the other *reactive*. The latter style makes available information about courses, conferences, post-graduate degrees and diplomas but does little or nothing in the way of organizing appropriate events. 'It is here if you want it—you must make the going.' I believe this is severely limited, because in a situation where the culture is still changing in terms of recognizing the importance of CME, it seems that the people who most need appropriate challenge and stimulus could be the ones whose CME grants lie unused year after year.

In my researches I came across considerable concern on the part of bishops and CME officers about the 'resistance' factor. One bishop identified essentially three types of clergy:

1. The *motivated*—the majority of whom are at the younger end of the age spectrum, recently ordained, conscious of being on a steep learning curve and of the need to keep up with changes in society and the church.
2. The *'middle-aged'*—not necessarily in years (!) but in attitude, content with 'keeping going,' in some instances counting the days to retirement.

---

15 Gerard Kelly, *Get a Grip on the Future…*, p 245.

3. The *freshly motivated*—people ordained having had a previous career, often high-calibre people who bring expertise and an expectation that 'in-service training' should be of equally high quality.

The bishop's comments indicated that the greatest need was to work with category 2, strengthening the role of CME as being something they would not want to miss out on.

Obviously, an imposed structure, is no better either: 'This is what "we" believe is good for you.' In Worcester Diocese, following the experience of several residential CME conferences being cancelled due to lack of interest, a new approach began with CME being linked to appraisal. Following an appraisal with a senior staff member, a tear-off sheet is sent to the Clergy Training Officer who will discuss the appropriate course of action for ongoing training and development. A similar situation exists in Rochester, where the Director of Ministry and Training will follow up the Review section on training outcomes.

In Blackburn Diocese, through the Director of Training, personal help and guidance has been offered for all clergy. This may be in an informal way or provided by a more structured form of consultancy. Particular consideration is given to five key stages of ministerial development: ordination or licensing; first incumbency; new post or change of responsibility; mid-service; pre-retirement. Bearing in mind clergy operate in an essentially 'flat' career structure, and sometimes get stuck because they have not had the opportunity to review their ministry at key points, it is good to know a number of dioceses now provide something like the above.

Interestingly, the Church of Scotland (arguably a church with an even 'flatter' structure) offers three-day conferences to its ministers to reflect on their ministry after 18 months, 5, 8 and 15 years in post. These consultations aim to help clergy to understand changing trends in society, to meet with others facing or working in similar situations and to think without pressure about where their ministry is going and whether or not any move would be appropriate.

In Hereford Diocese, where many clergy operate in isolated situations, there is a CME programme run jointly for clergy and readers which is often over-subscribed. 80% of the clergy attend one or more of the 10-15 training events each year. According to the Bishop of Ludlow, Dr John Saxbee, the reason for this is that people's isolation means that they value being with others and they experience the quality of input as being both high and relevant.

From my research, it seems clergy especially want input on:

- teamwork skills;
- collaborative ministry;
- discerning people's gifts;
- managing change;
- dealing with conflict;
- using new technology;
- interpreting the Bible today;

- the marginalization of the church;
- the role of the priest in a new century;
- approaches to appropriate worship in the local church;
- models of church for 'Generation Xers' and the Millennium generation.

Dioceses vary as to how much of a '3 line whip' operates as far as CME is concerned. Guildford Diocese, for example, requires clergy to be involved in at least one CME event per year and to use the remainder of their grant for something of their own personal choice. Surely this is a minimum requirement? Every other profession is (rightly) required to ensure in-service training is offered and completed—can we afford any less a commitment? But it must be high quality training and relevant to the participants.

A concern I had in hearing and reading about the various CME courses on offer was the evident danger of shying away from serious theological content. Somehow work needs to be done on bridging the gap between the theology taught as 'theory' at college and the realities of day to day church and parish life. We may be in a 'does it work?' rather than 'is it true?' mode in society but is that not all the more reason for a fresh approach to apologetics? A course in which I am involved as part of the teaching team seeks to bridge the gap, to engage both head and heart. Based at Cliff College near Sheffield, the Post-graduate Diploma in Leadership, Renewal and Mission Studies seeks to help practitioners from any denomination or stream to reflect theologically on their ministry in a changing world. Such a concern also lies behind John Reader's work on 'local theology'[16] with the role for the church being in the area of reason and rationality, because in the postmodern context the attack seems to be greater on reason than on tradition and revelation.

Alongside ongoing CME, most dioceses have a pattern of a residential clergy conference every 2, 3 or 4 years, for the inside of a week. As well as building the sense of value and belonging referred to earlier, at their best these can be important opportunities for learning and growth. As a variant to this pattern, Wakefield Diocese ran a series of smaller conferences in the 1990s which enabled groups of clergy to engage with a subject and each other over a three-day period.

Sabbaticals

If CME would have been an unfamiliar concept 20 years ago, by and large the concept of the sabbatical was unheard of! However, there is an increasing recognition that '...the forced productivity of both soil and soul make this ever more a necessity.'[17] Mindful of the sheer pace of life in today's world, most Dioceses are now encouraging 'time out' for clergy to enable reflection, re-creation, study and personal and spiritual nurture, based on the creation principle described in Genesis 2.2 plus an understanding of the Sabbath concept in Leviticus 25. To quote

16 See John Reader, *Local Theology* (Cardiff: Aureus, 1994).
17 Irvine, *Between Two Worlds* , p 165.

Guildford Diocese again, by 2001, they aim to make sabbaticals available 'as of right' building the costs of this into the diocesan budget. Sabbaticals usually last for three months, and are taken at 7- to 10-year intervals.

Having benefited from a first sabbatical after 26 years in ordained ministry, I now wonder why, when they are available, comparatively few clergy take up the opportunity. It may be they need a higher profile in a diocese and provision of pastoral cover and extra financial support may be required. There may also be a fear that the local church will resent or misunderstand the sabbatical: 'Why should s/he have this when the rest of us never get a break?' Fear of being 'out of role' may also figure highly for some. Although tired and conscious of the need to take serious time out, insecurity through this loss of role can feel quite acute. For many clergy it seems that their Christian security is bound up in what they are doing, rather than who they are in Christ.

My personal experience was that my sabbatical enabled me to refocus attention from such task orientation to find fresh intimacy with God, which in turn has helped me to re-establish a more balanced identity. (It could also be that 'modelling' sabbatical leave on the part of church leaders would not only benefit them but set a healthy trend in the pace and balance of life in the local church).

Ministerial Review

The majority of dioceses now have in place some kind of ministerial review. These vary in terms of methodology, frequency and aim. In contrast with the fear of and anger at 'being appraised' which was around a few years ago when the concept was first introduced, there is an understanding of this being a process to encourage not threaten. There is an increasing recognition that clergy must live responsibly with their vocation. This is why it is better that the word *review* rather than *appraisal* is used, since appraisal as used in other contexts is about monitoring performance, remuneration and career prospects. Rochester Diocese in the introduction to its *Ministry Review Handbook* expresses it thus:

> 'The Ministry Review scheme provides us with the regular opportunity to consider our calling and the practice of our own ministry. This is one of the ways in which we can become more open to renewal of our spirituality and our competence as servants and leaders of the churches where we serve.'

This seems to work best when members of the senior staff of a diocese are themselves involved in a review process. Thus, in Guildford, the diocesan bishop reviews his senior staff—suffragan bishop, archdeacons and heads of department, and he himself has a reviewer provided through the Archbishop of Canterbury's office.

Pastoral Provision

If it is in everyone's interests for the clergy as leaders of local church congregations to be valued, what pastoral support should be expected from the 'structures of the church' whether that means bishops, archdeacons or others of the senior staff?

My researches have indicated that whilst morale is relatively high among some clergy, for others a sense of uncertainty about their role, anxiety about money, problems with housing, worries about their family and safety issues leaves them feeling isolated and vulnerable and pastoral support is essential.

The general feeling is that crisis care from the 'hierarchy' is good though there is an understanding that, say, a 1 to 200 ratio of bishops to clergy means a limited possibility of *regular* pastoral contact. But the reality is many clergy do feel uncared for and maybe some of the crises that occur could be prevented by some kind of delegated responsibility for regular pastoral care.

When you consider that at somewhere like the London Lighthouse hospice every staff member is entitled to regular supervision, with the recognition that the maximum number reporting to an individual line-manager should be no more than seven, have not we got something to learn in the church? I believe each diocese should address these matters urgently, and that putting better pastoral provision in place would lead to a dramatic fall in sickness and burnout rates.

In his book *Who Ministers to Ministers?'* B Gilbert asks poignantly:

'Clergy and their spouses experience the same kind of joy, pain and broken-ness as their parishioners. Where do they turn when faced with personal problems?...Do they find the support they need?'[18]

It was good to hear of the counselling support network being developed in Lichfield Diocese, co-ordinated by their Adviser in Pastoral Care and Counsel-ling. The aim of this network is to provide a professional and confidential source of counselling for clergy and spouses. The first six sessions are free and thereafter subsidised rates can be negotiated. The aim is that this service should not simply be focussed on crisis times but should help with ongoing personal development.

Reflections from those who have used this service include:

'I see now that my ministry has been an avoidance of loneliness.'
'When I get it right for my family I feel I'm failing the parish and *vice versa*.'
'I cannot cope with taking more than four services on a Sunday.'
'I feel my ministry should be based on *being* and *holiness* but all the pressure is towards *management* and *success*.'
'The Church I have loved and served all my life has no place for my sexuality.'

It seems to me too there are some particular issues which need addressing as far as women's ministry is concerned. Within the Church of England, as with most churches, the clergy represent a male-dominated profession. Although of course many pastoral needs and concerns are shared in common by men and women,

18   B Gilbert, *Who Ministers to Ministers?* (New York: The Alban Institute) p 1.

there are for women some unique aspects and potential stress points to take into account. Some dioceses encourage women clergy to get together to share their experience of ministry—positive and negative. While there is at last evidence of women being taken seriously for senior posts, a lot of hurt has been caused where they have been considered in some way less than equal to the task. There is more to do in taking the role of women, and their pastoral needs, seriously.

Clergy have historically been trained or at least expected to cope with what-ever life throws at them and anything less than coping leads to shame and guilt. Whilst recognizing that pastoral support is not a single act, and needs to be devel-oped at various levels, including from the clergyperson's own initiative, it is right that there should be an expectation of input in this area from the 'official' struc-tures. Many clergy are sad that busyness in other areas squeezes out the role of the bishop as a prayerful leader, both for their sakes and for his.

5

Looking After Ourselves

'Self-denial is not the same as self-neglect…The world of action must decrease so the world of being can increase.' [19]

These were words which leapt off the page for me in the early weeks of my sab-batical in the summer of 1999. Throughout my ministry I have tried to put into practice the call from Jesus daily to 'deny yourself, take up your cross and follow me' (Luke 9.23). Stepping aside for a few weeks from what can feel to be the all-consuming nature of ministry, I came to see that indeed I had allowed self-denial to become self-neglect. Yes, for the minister as for every Christian there is a cost to be counted and difficulties and opposition to be faced, but should that be at the expense of our own well-being or that of those closest to us?

The Evangelical wing of the church in particular has been strong on this doc-trine of 'death to self' and I remember, as a curate, an experienced clergyman saying to me 'Never say "No" when a need presents itself'! At first hearing, this seems to accord entirely with Jesus' teaching about self-denial and self-giving—but it fails to accord with other instructions to his disciples, the future leaders of the church: 'Come apart by yourselves and rest awhile' (Mark 6.31).

When we add to this attitude the pressures faced by church leaders today, the expectations and perceptions of others, our own expectations of ourselves and the image created by the office or role, it is no wonder that many clergy suffer

[19] Irvine, *Between Two Worlds* , pp 107, 110.

from a lack of balance in their lives. The role becomes the primary identity—in order to function we adopt a particular persona. The 'outer' and 'inner' worlds of 'doing' and 'being' (to use the Jungian concepts) have got out of balance; we are driven to activism and have forgotten who we truly are.

A fresh look at the life and ministry of Jesus can give us the basis to rediscover who we are, how we can look after ourselves and how we can seek to live a more balanced, integrated life in the world, being glad to embrace our own humanity.

Perhaps what many clergy need is permission, and maybe help and guidance, to seek this sense of integration, to nurture their 'inner world' and, in an appropriate way, replicate Jesus' approach to life. As St Paul wrote, 'Let this mind be in you that was also in Christ Jesus' (Philippians 2.5). When we look carefully, as we have noted already, we see in Jesus someone who submitted to his Father's will, as he took time apart to pray, yet did not neglect his physical or emotional needs. He developed significant relationships with his disciples and those who were closest to him.

I suggest these three dimensions of Jesus' life and ministry—the Father's will, his own needs and relationships with others—might give us a checklist, a tool kit that ensures not just survival but growth, bearing in mind as Henri Nouwen has written, 'Ministry can be fruitful only if it grows out of a direct and intimate encounter with our Lord.'[20]

1. Submitting to the Father's Will

Knowing the guilt that can immediately assail clergy as well as other Christians when it comes to reflecting on our own spiritual lives, it seems to me what clergy need is a spirituality that both sustains and empowers effective leadership and ministry. We need a realistic expectation of ourselves, combined with an appropriate 'growing' spirituality.

If the crucial factor in the effectiveness of the local church is the quality of its spirituality, which can be defined as our understanding of how encounter with God takes place and how such an encounter is sustained, then what is going on or not going on for its leaders will be of enormous significance.

In this 'transition' time for church, society and the role and identity of the clergy, what is realistically available to help us experience growth and development in our spirituality? Riddell says: 'When the heart is captivated by Christ, then all of existence becomes a resource for growing in depth and understanding.'[21] This speaks of a rediscovery of who we are in Christ—a reminder of Jesus' call to the first disciples to *be* with him as well as go in his name. Part of this rediscovery may reveal a need to let go of a distorted view of the Father's will and his expectations of us. How we understand and see God will affect the way we live. A demanding God leads to a driven ministry—and there is much evidence of this around. The opposite extreme, of course, is a perception of a God who

---

20 Henri Nouwen, *The Way of the Heart* (London: DLT, 1981) p 31.
21 Riddell, *Threshold of the Future*, p 143.

makes no demands; this can lead to a ministry that lacks direction and purpose.

We can ourselves take a number of deliberate steps to develop a more accurate view of the Father's will and purpose.

a) A Visiting, or Revisiting, of the 'Spiritual Disciplines'

Richard Foster believes that it is the classical disciplines of prayer, meditation, Bible study, simplicity, solitude, submission, service, confession, worship, guidance and celebration that can promote a deep inner life, *'drawing us inward into the transformation we need,'* and hearing *'the call outward into the ministry we need: healing the sick, suffering with the broken, interceding for the world.'* [22]

There will need to be a conscious commitment to making this a priority. It will not happen 'by drift.' Again, to quote Nouwen, 'It is from the transformed or converted self that real ministry flows.'[23] It may mean honestly asking ourselves tough questions, like:

- What occurs in my life that nurtures me spiritually?
- What occupies the space at the centre of my life?
- What drives and motivates me?

b) Keeping a Spiritual Journal

It was my spiritual director who encouraged me in this discipline many years ago and, to be honest, intention has won the day over reality for much of that time. But again during my sabbatical time when there were no other excuses dressed up as reasons in the way, I began to keep a journal on an almost daily basis. I have continued this since returning to work. Sometimes it is just a page reflecting on the key moments and encounters, positive and negative, of the previous day. At other times, it will include reflection on my Bible reading or devotional book. Also included are prayers for others and for whatever might be in the news. I find it is a helpful part of the process of enabling me to prioritize and organize my life and ministry more effectively.

It *is* a discipline—but I have begun to realize that without this or its equivalent, spiritual growth becomes indiscernible except in the broadest terms. What may be difficult to start with becomes an invaluable part of life. It is also exciting and faith-building to look back and see how God resolved an apparently intractable situation. But to prevent it becoming burdensome, keep it simple!

c) Bible Study and Prayer

The Anglican Ordinal has the bishop ask those he is about to ordain:

'Will you be diligent in prayer, in reading holy Scripture and in all studies that will deepen your faith and fit you to uphold the truth of the gospel *against error?*' [24]

---

22   R Foster, *Prayer* (Sevenoaks: Hodder and Stoughton, 1992) p 273.
23   Henri Nouwen, *The Way of the Heart* , p 20.
24   *The Anglican Ordinal—The Alternative Service Book* (Oxford: Mowbray, 1980) p 373.

The ordained are accountable—but who asks questions or gives support in these areas? It is firstly, I believe, in the clergy's own hands to take responsibility for personal spiritual growth.

Again, we need to ask ourselves questions like:

• How, and how often, do we study the Bible?
• What prevents fruitful personal Bible study?

Often, ironically, it is preparation for preaching and teaching that gets in the way of fruitful personal Bible study—though for some with a particular teaching gift this is not the case. The one clearly feeds the other.

Every working life has its rhythms of demands and energy and the working lives of those in full-time ministry are no exception, so it is good to recognize the need for and build in seasons of greater potential study for Bible reading and prayer, when we have more time and energy, to compensate for times when this is less possible.

Dr John Stott in *I Believe in Preaching* recommends an overall rhythm of an hour a day, a day a month and a week a year set aside for personal Bible study and prayer.[25] In my experience the hour a day is the hardest to hold on to, yet maybe we can move from being 'too busy to pray and study' to being 'too prayerful to be as busy' and prioritize the time apart with God.

d) Spiritual Director/Professional Support

Although we are, at the end of the day, responsible for our own spiritual growth and nurture, it would seem either arrogant or naive to think we can manage without input or guidance from others. I believe that every Christian leader should have someone, whether a 'spiritual director' or 'soul friend' who can be such a resource person in their lives. Clergy are those who take on board others' needs and struggles. Dare we be so caught up with this that we neglect the need for someone, outside the local church structures, to give us space, for both support and challenge? This is especially important at the beginning of ministry and at times of transition or changes of responsibility.

How exactly this relationship works out will vary from person to person. My own personal experience of having had such input over more than 20 years is that seeing a spiritual director 4 or 5 times a year, with the knowledge that they can be contacted at other times *in extremis* is about right. Rev David Charles-Edwards, a management consultant and part-time stipendiary priest, who has worked both in secular and church contexts, observes that many clergy have no effective support or challenge from 'outside.' He would argue that, as people involved in dealing regularly with serious and demanding pastoral situations, there should be professional supervision every six to eight weeks. The Diocese of Lichfield have been exploring the possibility of providing this facility. In a pilot study in two

25 See J R W Stott, *I Believe in Preaching* (London: Hodder and Stoughton, 1982).

deaneries, clergy have had access to this kind of professional supervision at that frequency for one-and-half hours at a time. On an ongoing basis, such support would have financial implications—but, again, if the clergy are the church's most significant asset, can we afford *not* to provide such support?

Another model, from the Diocese of Blackburn, is that of a 'Pastoral Companion,' offered as a facility for clergy and their spouses. A mix of lay and ordained, female and male have been trained to fulfil this role of sharing the journey of faith and ministry.

Action
- Commit one regular piece of your time—a morning or evening a week—to re-rooting your relationship with God.
- Start to keep a spiritual journal.
- Enquire about the possibility of a spiritual director or companion, if you do not have one already.

---

2. Recognizing Our Human Needs
a) Physical needs

These needs must be met, but are often the first to be neglected. We overwork, get over-intense, maybe overeat, or drink too much, neglecting exercise and rest. Again, we have misunderstood some words of Jesus: 'My Father is always working and *I am always working*' (John 5.17). Thus clergy justify taking little or no time off. Apart from the fact that our bodies are 'temples of the Holy Spirit,' we have a responsibility to ourselves and to those close to us to take care of ourselves.

Often it seems it is only when severe warning bells have rung that we take any action. A clergyman I knew in Cumbria, who had experienced a near-fatal heart attack, took an hour's exercise around lunchtime each day and if anyone came to see him then, they either had to wait or walk with him! He had learned to take responsibility for his physical well-being and that exercise became part of his daily life.

Action
If overall health allows, commit to regular exercise each week, whether a weekly walk in the countryside or somewhere nearby in your lunch hour. Experience the slower pace of a pedestrian and be open to what is around you. Take time out in whatever way helps the relaxation process.

---

b) Intellectual needs

We need to continue to grow and develop intellectually, both in ongoing theological reflection so that our book shelves do not betray when we 'died' theologically, but also as we engage with the issues of this changing world. If that sounds like yet another pressure to 'keep up our reading' and it seems we cannot afford the time in this way, I want again to ask—can we afford not to?

A person who is not committed to this kind of life-long learning is in danger of functioning on yesterday's thoughts, which is neither good for them nor those whom they lead and to whom they preach. David Fisher has advised that 'we need to become expert at reading and understanding cultural maps.'[26] Gerard Kelly suggests that 'twenty-first century leaders will find themselves constantly asking, "What have I learned today...this week...this year?"'[27]

Action
- Have a reading week once a year, or two 3 day sessions a year.
- Take a day a month 'thinking time.'
- Join an evening class—local university or college—on literature, history, philosophy or sociology.
- Join a local film society or club.
- Subscribe to a magazine covering an area about which you know little but which is significant in today's world.

---

3. Significant Relationships

We all know that relationships are a paradox—they bring us the greatest joy and the greatest pain. Because relationships are a major source of stress for clergy, we also need ones that can nurture and support. Far too many clergy interact at levels that leave a deep sense of personal unfulfilment.

A ministry modelled on that of Jesus will always be relational. Recognizing that systems and structures cannot and should not be expected to provide everything, I believe clergy need to take responsibility for developing significant and supportive relationships, creating opportunities for personal support. (Within this I recognize that some personality types will find this harder than others.)

This can happen at three levels: within the local church; with other clergy or ministers; and beyond the church community.

a) Within the Local Church

I believe the concept of clergy as non-relational beings, in the sense of having no significant relationships in the local church, betrays a bad theology. There is indeed a sense of being 'set apart' but as we read the New Testament letters of Paul and John in particular we see many references to close and significant relationships, not least as evidenced by the greetings contained within them.

Of course there is risk in this. My father's generation (he served in ordained ministry from 1946–1974) were taught to have no friends in the local church because of the dangers of favouritism and to have no further contact after leaving a

26   David Fisher, *The 21st Century Pastor* (Zondervan, 1996) quoted in *Netfax* 49, The Leadership Network, 8 July 1996, http://www.leadnet.ord
27   Gerard Kelly, *Get a Grip on the Future...*, p 246.

parish. For similar reasons the Salvation Army used to have 2 years maximum appointments and Methodist ministers 5 years maximum. Of course we must take care to treat people for whom we are responsible evenhandedly, and there is always a risk of misinterpretation. But Jesus was a great risk-taker and boundary crosser and, as we see from the gospels, chose to share significant moments with Peter, James and John. The risk of having no significant relationships is that it leads to an increase in the sense of separation and isolation, both for clergy and their spouses, and is damaging to personal development as well as to an effective ministry.

Action
    Seek out 2 or 3 people in your local church whom you have learned are trustworthy; ask them to pray for you after each service and/or meet with you at frequent intervals. Share your heart with them. (Not strategy—that belongs in other places, but who and how you are.)

---

b) With other Clergy or Ministers:
    Fraternals, chapters and clergy fellowships can sometimes be superficial, tedious, turgid and competitive rather than collaborative. Very often the agenda is concerned with no more than planning programmes or events, and it can be difficult to share and discuss at a more personal level. Steve Croft, in his book *Ministry in Three Dimensions*[28] suggests that about half the time in clergy staff meetings, chapters and fraternals should be given to sharing and study, and the other half to business.

Action
- Challenge the level of contact and expectations in your local Chapter or fellowship.
- Begin to disclose personal need; tell some stories of both heartache and encouragement.
- Party together, meet socially with spouses.

Peer support: 'Support' is not a single act but needs to operate in various ways, so clergy need to develop support on multiple levels, one of which could be peer support. In the Diocese of Guildford there are examples of six or eight clergy from an area getting together on a regular basis. Similarly, in Lichfield Diocese, there is growing encouragement for clergy to be part of informal clusters. Another model that some Dioceses operate is gathering people together around the common factor they share in ministry contexts: inner-city, rural, urban and suburban, multi-

---

28   See Steve Croft, *Ministry in Three Dimensions* (London: SPCK, 1999).

faith, problems and opportunities of large churches, the limitations and possibilities for smaller churches.

Action
   Which of the above suggestions might I be able to be part of or encourage to develop?

---

c) Beyond the Church Community

Social activity beyond the local church which is work-related is fine—but we need something more, something different to enrich our lives. To the charge 'I haven't time,' again I would respond 'Can we afford not to?' Relationships and relaxation outside the church context help us to get a different, wider view of life. It can help to restore perspective and remind us that we are in the kingdom business which is bigger than local church leadership.

We live in an age of 'delayed responsibility.' Credit card use is at an all-time high; we plan to start dieting and exercising and reviewing our spiritual life 'tomorrow,' but we have had these plans for the last year—or more! Jesus said we are to love our neighbours *as ourselves* and part of that looking after ourselves might mean getting a grip on some of the inner chaos and outward pressures—for our own sakes and that of our ministries.

Henri Nouwen again has some wisdom for us:

'We have indeed to fashion our own desert where we can withdraw every day, shake off our compulsions and dwell in the gentle healing presence of our Lord. Without such a desert we will lose our own soul while preaching the gospel to others...Ministry can be fruitful only if it grows out of a direct and intimate encounter with our Lord.'[29]

---

29   H Nouwen, *The Way of the Heart* , p 30.

6
Dreams That Could Become Reality

It was on the 28th August 1963 that Martin Luther King uttered these now fa-
mous words—'I have a dream'—concerning the way civil rights for black people
as well as white people could become reality in the United States of America.
Some five years later, he paid for that vision with his life.

What we have been concerned with in this book is of course not on the same
scale as King's vision. Nevertheless, to my mind, there is a responsibility on both
the structures of the church as represented by a Diocese or its equivalent, the local
church and each individual clergyperson to make what might still be dreams a
reality. What is needed is more than just a strategy for survival; we need an emerg-
ing environment that embodies hope.

The check-list below is a mixture of what already is (at least in some places!)
and what might be. I dream of a church in which:

- Every clergyperson has a 'safe place' where they can be listened to and prayed
  for on a regular basis;
- Professional supervision/work consultancy/mentoring is regularly available
  (perhaps every 6–8 weeks) and paid for by the diocese and local church;
- Every clergyperson is actively encouraged to seek a spiritual director;
- There is appropriately tailored CME with particular input on teamwork and
  collaborative ministry for laity and clergy together, courses being regularly
  available in or shared between dioceses;
- Good practice is learned from other organizations with expertise in volunteer-
  ing and the support of paid workers in a volunteer-intensive organization;
- Sabbaticals are available for all clergy every 7 to 10 years, with the expectation
  of them being taken up unless there is good reason otherwise;
- Personal and ministerial reviews for all clergy take place on a regular basis (at
  least once a year);
- Regular pastoral care for clergy, their spouses and families is made available
  and accessible;
- Clergy, in addition to a day off each week and an annual retreat, are encour-
  aged to have at least half a day personal review time each week and monthly
  study and thinking days;
- At least every 5 to 7 years there is the opportunity for clergy to attend a 'Stages
  of Ministry' conference.

I could add more, but if only some of this imagined future became a reality, the
highest number of ordinands currently in training in the Church of England for
30 years would be better supported. There would be ongoing resources for their
ministry, in a church that demonstrates a support-literate culture.